A Multi-Skills Activity Book

interactions one

Emily Austin Thrush
The University of Memphis

Deborah Poole
San Diego State University

McGraw Hill

Boston, Massachusetts   Burr Ridge, Illinois   Dubuque, Iowa
Madison, Wisconsin   New York, New York   San Francisco, California   St. Louis, Missouri

McGraw-Hill

*A Division of The **McGraw·Hill** Companies*

This is an  book

Interactions One

A Multi-Skills Activity Book

domestic   1 2 3 4 5 6 7 8 9 0 DOC DOC 9 0 0 9 8 7 6
international   1 2 3 4 5 6 7 8 9 0 DOC DOC 9 0 0 9 8 7 6

ISBN 0-07-050338-9

Editorial Director: Thalia Dorwick
Publisher: Tim Stookesberry
Sponsoring editor: Tim Stookesberry
Development editor: Bill Preston
Marketing manager: Andy Martin
Production supervisor: Florence Fong
Designers: Lorna Lo, Suzanne Montazer, Francis Owens, and Elizabeth Williamson
Cover designer: Francis Owens
Cover illustrator: Susan Pizzo
Photo Researcher: Elyse Rieder
Editorial Assistant: Brett Glass
Compositor: Chris Boyer and Associates
Typeface: Times Roman
Printer: R.R. Donnelly & Sons Company, Crawsfordsville, IN

International Edition

When ordering this title, use ISBN 0-07-114377-7.

http://www.mhhe.com

(continued on page 194)

Contents

Preface   vii

School Life   1

Reading: *One Student's Life: Tan Nguyen*   3
Watching a Video: "ESL Students in New York"   7
Listening/Speaking: Comparing School Services   6
Writing: Writing About School Life   9

Experiencing Nature   11

Reading: *The World of Nature*   13, *Save Our Bear*   18
Watching a Video: "Samson the Bear"   18
Listening/Speaking: Conducting a Debate: The Airport vs. the Wetlands   22
Writing: Writing a Postcard   16, Writing About Samson   21, Writing About the Debate   25

Living to Eat or Eating to Live?   29

Reading: *The Four Basic Food Groups*   32, *The Great American Diet*   39
Watching a Video: "Fast Food and Fat"   36

Listening/Speaking: Discussing Your Diet 35
Writing: Writing About Fast Food 43, Writing About Diets 36

CHAPTER**four**

Getting Around the Community

45

Reading: *Communities in the United States* 48, *A "Local Hero" in Miami* 54
Watching a Video: " A Cultural Celebration" 51
Listening/Speaking: Community Role Play 53
Writing: Writing a Letter of Request 57, Writing About Predictions 59

CHAPTER**five**

Home

61

Reading: *House for Sale?* 63, *Apartment Ads* 71
Watching a Video: "Buying a Home" 67
Listening/Speaking: Describing Your Dream House or Apartment 74
Writing: Writing About Homes 66, Writing a Letter 75

CHAPTER**six**

Emergencies and Strange Experiences

77

Reading: *Natural Disasters* 78, *Fire Facts* 87, *Preventing Fires* 88
Watching a Video: "An Earthquake in Japan" 84
Listening/Speaking: Talking About Emergencies 82,
   Preparing for Emergency Situations 91
Writing: Writing About Natural Disasters 86, Writing About Emergency Situations 94

CHAPTER seven

Health

97

Reading: *Health Issues* 99
Watching a Video: "The 'Flu' and Flu Shots" 106
Listening/Speaking: Talking About Stress 109
Writing: Writing to a Health Expert 108, Writing About Stress 112

CHAPTER eight

Entertainment and the Media

115

Reading: *Video on Demand* 118
Watching a Video: "Interactive TV" 120
Listening/Speaking: Discussing Television 122
Writing: Writing About Interactive TV 120, Keeping a Television Ratings Dairy 125, Writing About Your Favorite TV Show 127

CHAPTER nine

Social Life

129

Reading: *Helping Love Along: College Park Dating Service* 132, *Newlyweds: Reluctance Turns To Romance* 144
Watching a Video: "Finding a Mate" 135
Listening/Speaking: Discussing Friends 137, Making a Short Speech 139
Writing: Giving Advice 140, Writing About a Wedding 145

CHAPTER ten

Customs, Celebrations, and Holidays

147

Reading: *Celebrations and the Multicultural Society* 149
Watching a Video: "A Cultural Celebration" 151
Listening/Speaking: Making a Poster Presentation 156, Discussing Holidays 157
Writing: Writing About Holidays 158

CHAPTER eleven

Science and Technology

161

Reading: *The Great Multimedia Debacle* 164
Watching a Video: "CD-ROMs" 167
Listening/Speaking: Designing a Multimedia CD-ROM 170
Writing: Writing About New Technology 167, Writing a Proposal Letter 170

CHAPTER twelve

You, the Consumer

173

Reading: *Spender or Saver?* 175, *Using a Consumer Guide* 184
Watching a Video: "Shopping" 178
Listening/Speaking: Interviewing and Taking a Poll 181, Role Play 182
Writing: Writing About Shopping 180, Writing a Recommendation 186

Answer Key 189

Preface

The Interactions One Program

The Interactions One program consists of five texts and a variety of supplemental materials for high-beginning to low-intermediate students seeking to improve their English language skills. Each of the five texts in this program is carefully organized by chapter theme, vocabulary, grammar structures, and, where possible, language functions. As a result, information introduced in a chapter of any one of the Interactions One texts corresponds to and reinforces material taught in the same chapter of the other four books, creating a truly integrated, four-skills approach.

The Interactions One program is highly flexible. The texts in this series may be used together or separately, depending on students' needs and course goals. The books in this program include:

- **A Communicative Grammar Book.** Organized around grammatical topics, this book includes notional/functional material where appropriate. It presents all grammar in context and contains many types of communicative activities.

- **A Listening/Speaking Skills Book.** This book uses lively, natural language from various contexts, including dialogues, interviews, lectures, and announcements. Listening strategies emphasized include summarizing main ideas, making inferences, listening for stressed words, reductions, and intonation. A variety of speaking skills complement the listening component.

- **A Reading Skills Book.** The reading selections contain sophisticated college-level material; however, vocabulary and grammar have been carefully controlled to be at students' level of comprehension. The text includes many vocabulary-building exercises and emphasizes reading strategies such as skimming, scanning, guessing meaning from context, understanding the structure and organization of a selection, increasing reading speed, and interpreting the author's point of view.

- **A Writing Process Book.** This book uses a process approach to writing, including many exercises on prewriting and revision. Exercises build skills in exploring and organizing ideas; developing vocabulary; using correct form and mechanics; using coherent structure, and editing, revising, and using feedback to create a final draft.

- **A Multi-Skills Activity Book.** New to this edition, this text gives students integrated practice in all four language skills. Among the communicative activities included in this text are exercises for the new video program that accompanies the Interactions One series.

Supplemental Materials

In addition to the five core texts outlined above, various supplemental materials are available to assist users of the third edition, including:

Instructor's Manual

Extensively revised for the new edition, this manual provides instructions and guidelines for using the five core texts separately or in various combinations to suit particular program needs. There is a separate section with answer keys, teaching tips, additional activities, and other suggestions. The testing materials have been greatly expanded in this edition.

Audio Program for Interactions One: A Listening/Speaking Skills Book

Completely re-recorded for the new edition, the audio program is designed to be used in conjunction with those exercises that are indicated with a cassette icon in the student text. Complete tapescripts are now included in the back of the student text.

Audio Program to Accompany Interactions One:
A Reading Skills Book

This new optional audio program contains selected readings from the student text. These taped selections of poems, articles, stories, and speeches enable students to listen at their leisure to the natural oral discourse of native readers for intonation and modeling. Readings that are included in this program are indicated with a cassette icon in the student text.

Video

New to this edition, the video program for Interactions One contains authentic television segments that are coordinated with the twelve chapter themes in the five texts. Exercises and activities for this video are in the Multi-Skills Activity Book.

Interactions One: A Multi-Skills Activity Book

Rationale

Interactions One: A Multi-Skills Activity Book provides an opportunity for students to integrate the language skills covered in the other books in the Interactions series. Each chapter offers lessons and exercises in the language skill areas of reading, speaking, listening and writing. These activities are all related to the chapter theme and are integrated with each other. For example, the reading activities prepare students for listening to the video. Together, the reading and listening exercises lead to the speaking activities that follow, which in turn help students prepare to do the writing assignment for the chapter.

This book is based on units of theme-based language instruction. In this approach to language teaching, students have a chance to practice the language related to a given topic in all skill areas. In this way, learning within one skill supports learning in the others. So, for example, the grammar and vocabulary that a student is exposed to through a listening activity may be encountered again through reading or speaking lessons, and then incorporated into a writing assignment. By bringing all skills together in relation to one theme or topic, students have repeated and varied exposure to the language needed for competence within a given topic domain. In addition, they have a range of situations in which to practice the language they learn.

Chapter Organization

Interactions One: A Multi-Skills Activity Book consists of twelve chapters. Each chapter has a central theme. The twelve chapter themes correspond to those in the other four books in the Interactions One program.

The lessons and activities in this book are designed to be "meaning-focused" and to provide students with authentic communicative situations which will allow for language development through negotiation and problem-solving. They are also carefully structured to allow students to practice and master language associated with the theme. However, this book does not contain many explicit grammar exercises. We believe, however, that form-focused material used in conjunction with this book will be of great benefit to students. We recommend using *Interactions One: A Communicative Grammar,* Third Edition; grammar topics presented and practiced in detail in that text correspond to and expand upon grammar topics that appear in this multi-skills book.

The readings are particularly important in leading into the other sections; research shows that all language skills are improved when students read at an appropriate level for their language ability. The readings also help develop the students' schema, or background knowledge, for the other sections. The sections are carefully sequenced in each chapter to build language skills in an effective and interesting way; we encourage teachers to follow the sequence as closely as possible to get maximum benefit from the integration of skills in this texts.

Teaching Suggestions

Videotape Segments

An important and exciting feature of *Interactions One: A Multi-Skills Activity Book* is the use of video lessons designed to teach listening comprehension. Each video segment is related to the chapter theme and is taken from a local TV news program in San Diego, California, or New York City (USA). The video lessons offer teachers and students several features that can enhance the teaching of listening:

- short stretches of authentic, unsimplified spoken English that can be reviewed several times to increase comprehension

- lots of visual and graphic information that can aid students' comprehension of the spoken language

- text activities designed to help students comprehend the most important general information and some of the specific details

- situations that illustrate numerous cultural features of the United States

Working with Videotapes

The Interactions One video segments and the activities that accompany them are designed to help students comprehend natural spoken English. When you work with the video exercises to practice listening, it is important to keep several things in mind:

1. Perhaps most importantly, students should not be expected to understand every word. Because the tapes use authentic speech samples, the activities are designed to help students understand as much as they can *without* having 100% comprehension.

2. The pre-listening discussions or vocabulary preview activities are very important teaching tools to help students understand as much as possible. By doing these activities, students will develop expectations about what they will see on the video, as well as gaining background knowledge and language relevant to the topic. You may also want to develop some of your own preparation activities. Be sure to preview each video before showing it to your class. This way, you can better prepare your students to watch and listen.

3. The activities for each video clip have been carefully sequenced to allow for more than one viewing. In all cases, the first viewing encourages listening for gist or general information, and the second (and sometimes third) guides students to comprehend more specific information.

4. Although all of the video clips are short (between 2 and 5 minutes), you may find that it helps students to stop the tape once or twice during some of the longer segments.

Using the Writing Activities

Many writing texts, whether for native or non-native speakers of English, currently take a process approach to writing instruction. In brief, the writing process includes the following stages:

1. **Invention.** Activities that help students generate content include brainstorming, free writing, listing, dialoguing, visualizing, and the use of various graphic organizers, such as Venn diagrams and tree charts.

2. **Analysis of Audience and Purpose.** Students answer questions about the intended reader(s) and purpose(s) to guide them toward appropriate choices of vocabulary, sentence structure, format, and, perhaps, graphics.

3. **Drafting.** Students develop the ideas generated in the invention phase by determining a plan of organization, and adding details, examples, analogies, illustrations, anecdotes, and other types of evidence. At this stage, students build paragraphs, going from specific to general or general to specific, using narration or spatial development, comparing and contrasting, showing cause and effect, adding definitions, and developing their arguments.

4. **Peer Reviewing.** Guided by sets of questions and criteria, students look at each others' writing, reacting to it as the intended reader might, and making suggestions for improving content, clarity, and organization. They may also provide help with mechanics: spelling, punctuation, grammar, and format.

5. **Revising.** Working from the comments of the peer reviewers and the teacher, students revise their drafts.

The peer review and revision stages can be repeated, resulting in multiple drafts that come closer and closer in approximation to the ideal. The amount of input by the teacher varies, depending on the ability of the students as writers and peer reviewers. The ultimate goal, of course, is for the students to be able to use the resources available to them to write well and effectively, without the necessity of help from an English teacher.

In Chapter Seven of *Interactions One: A Multi-Skills Activity Book,* the writing task on pages 112–114 includes five activities for applying the writing process approach; other chapters include only the writing assignment. Because writing is just one of the four basic skills addressed and integrated in this activity book, it is left to the teacher to determine how much emphasis to give to the writing process. For more extensive information on using the writing process approach, please see *Interactions One: A Writing Process Book,* Third Edition.

Using Small Group and Pair Work

Small group and pair work has become common in language classrooms because of the benefits these types of activities afford students, including:

- creation of a comfortable atmosphere for language practice that is more like natural conversation and less like testing or performing

- more speaking opportunities for all students, including those who are reluctant to speak up in front of a large class

- more chances for repetition, clarification, and questioning

- a change in teacher-student interaction, freeing the teacher to move around the room and work with groups and individuals as they need assistance

- a chance for students to use their language skills in a more authentic, communicative, interactive context

Getting Started with Small Group Work

Small group activities will be easier to introduce to your classes if you:

- choose tasks in which the language is controlled and adjusted to the abilities of your students (if they are in the minimal production stage, for example, activities should call for one or two-word responses)

- begin with short activities (no longer than 5–10 minutes)

- begin with pair work and expand to small groups when your students are comfortable working together

General Principles for Small Group Work

The following principles are vitally important to making small group work successful:

1. Make the task clear and focused so that students will understand what they are doing and experience success doing it. (Try not to cram three projects into one work activity.)

2. Pay attention to the seating arrangement: Students need to be sitting so that they face each other.

3. Explain the purpose of the activity as well as the directions for doing it. What does it have to do with the purpose of the course? How will participating in this task contribute to, for example, completing the next writing assignment?

4. Make sure directions are clear. Ask students to explain back to you what they are supposed to do before they begin the activity.

5. Circulate around the room during the activity to help students who have problems and to answer questions, being careful not to intrude when you're not needed.

6. Monitor for whole group participation. If each student seems to be working alone, for example, consider how the task can be restructured to ensure more collaboration (e.g., require reaching consensus in the group, ask each group to select a recorder who will record the group input, if a form is used, require that each student write the same thing on the form, etc.)

7. Set clear time limits and stick to them. If activities drag on too long, students will lose interest in them. If students are not finished with the task at the end of the time limit you set, extend the time briefly, announcing the extension to the students. This lets them know that:

   • they aren't going to be in this group forever;

   • you as teacher are still in control;

   • you are going to resume the teacher role.

8. Include a whole class follow-up activity. This should include feedback from you which ratifies or corrects the work completed. There are a variety of ways this can be done:

   • Have a student reporter report from each group, orally or on the board.

   • Summarize, or elicit summaries from the groups, possibly using the overhead projector or board to display the results.

   • Discuss key points or problems observed (e.g., with grammar).

A Step Beyond the Classroom

At the end of each chapter are suggested activities designed take students outside the classroom. These activities will be most useful if you are teaching in an English speaking environment. Many of these activities include interviews, phone conversations, newspapers, or field trips. We believe that drawing on the out-of-class environment will make the language acquisition process more rapid while affording students opportunities to connect with the communities where they reside.

We hope that those instructors in non-English speaking areas will take full advantage of the English resources that are available, such as English-language newspapers; American, British, Canadian, or Australian companies or high schools; and English-speaking tourists or residents. These are all resources that can be effectively tapped by your students. Taking advantage of these resources will expose your students to many contexts of natural language use that cannot be duplicated inside the classroom, and we would encourage any adaptation of our activities that would make this feasible. Also, some activities might be done in the students' native languages so that the information they gather can be brought back to the classroom and discussed or written about in English.

INTERACTIONS ONE: A Multi-Skills Activity Book

CHAPTER **one**

School Life

in this chapter

You will talk about student life at your school, including various school services. You will read about a Vietnamese student's life at a community college and watch a short video about college students from the former Soviet Union in New York City. Finally, you will write about your own life at school.

Getting Ready

activity one

Warming Up

Which of the following statements describe your life as a student? In the blank next to each sentence, write <u>yes</u>, <u>no</u>, or <u>sometimes</u>. Then, talk about your answers with your class or in small groups.

1. _____ I like the classes that I am taking.

2. _____ I am learning a lot in my classes.

3. _____ I have made new friends at school.

4. _____ I don't understand everything that my teachers say.

5. _____ I don't understand everything in my textbooks.

6. _____ At school, I know where to get help for different kinds of problems.

7. _____ I don't have enough time to study.

8. _____ I have a job for more than eight hours a week.

9. _____ My classes will help me reach my goals for the future.

10. _____ I'd rather be working full-time than going to school.

activity two

Comparing Your Answers

As a class, figure out how many students answered <u>yes</u> or <u>no</u> to each question. Make a chart on the board to show how the class answered the questions.

Reading About School Life

Reading

Read the following story about Tan Nguyen. Think about these questions as you read: How is your school life similar to his? How is it different?

One Student's Life: Tan Nguyen

A   Tan Nguyen is a student at Mountain View Community College. He is taking English as a Second Language (ESL) classes there twelve hours a week. He also takes one math class.

B   Tan is a hard-working student, and he is very busy. He has a job working twenty hours per week at a computer software company, and sometimes he doesn't have enough time to study. It is important for him to work because he helps to support his parents and younger brothers and sisters.

C   Tan plans to get a degree in engineering from the state university. He really wants to study computer science, but he thinks his English isn't good enough. His friends told him that he doesn't need to have very good English to major in electrical engineering (EE), so he's going to major in EE.

D   After this semester, Tan can take freshman composition. The college has another semester of ESL, but it isn't required, and Tan doesn't want to take it. He needs to finish ESL quickly because it takes so much time. His parents want him to finish his education so that he can bring more money into the family.

Understanding the Reading

activity one

Exploring Words

Find and circle the following words in the story. What do you think they mean? Talk about them with your teacher and classmates.

community college   electrical engineering

engineering   major

degree   freshman composition

state university   semester

computer science   required

activity two

Working with Third Person Singular

In each sentence, circle the correct verb form to make a true statement about Tan Nguyen.

1. Tan Nguyen has/doesn't have a job at a restaurant.

2. Tan works/doesn't work twenty hours a week.

3. He helps/doesn't help support his family.

4. He wants/doesn't want to major in electrical engineering.

5. He wants/doesn't want to take another semester of ESL.

activity three

Discussing the Reading

Work in small groups. Discuss the following questions about the reading. For each question, write down the number of students in your group who answer <u>yes</u> and the number who answer <u>no</u>. Choose one person to report your group's discussion to the whole class.

1. Do you think Tan made a good decision about his major?

    Yes _____   No _____

    Why or why not? _____

    _____

2. Do you think most parents think the same way as Tan's?

Yes _____   No _____

Why or why not? _____

_____

3. Do you think Tan should take one more semester of ESL?

Yes _____   No _____

Why or why not? _____

_____

4. Do you think the college should require ESL?

Yes _____   No _____

Why or why not? _____

_____

activity four

Writing a Letter

Write a short letter to Tan Nguyen. Tell him what you think about his decision about his major. Use the model below to help you get started.

_____
(Today's Date)

Dear Mr. Nguyen:

In my class we read about you. I think you made a _____

decision about your major because _____

_____

_____

_____

_____

Yours truly,

_____
(Your signature here)

Learning About School Services

activity five

1. Most schools have different kinds of services to help students. Find a catalog about your school and read about the services that it offers. Then form small groups and answer the following questions.

   - What services does your school have?
   - Where are they and what do they do?
   - Which ones do you use?

2. Use the catalog from step 1 above. Fill in the chart below. When you finish, form small groups and compare your answers. Then discuss your answers with your teacher and the whole class.

Using Your School Services				
	Does your school have a(n) _____?	Do you know where it is?	Have you used it?	What services does it offer?
tutoring center				
writing center				
counseling center				
advising office				
health center				
library				
admissions office				
financial aid office				
gymnasium				

Writing a Letter

activity six

Write a letter to one of the school services on the chart. Ask for information about the services that they offer.

INTERACTIONS ONE: A Multi-Skills Activity Book

Watching a Video
"ESL Students in New York"

Preparing to Watch

activity one

You are going to watch a short video about college students in New York City. The students are from the former Soviet Union. Before you watch, find a partner and discuss the words below. Put a check (✔) beside the ones you know. Then discuss the words you don't know with your teacher and classmates.

_____	Brooklyn	_____	college course
_____	Long Island	_____	life skills
_____	intensive English study	_____	major
_____	language labs	_____	pharmacy
_____	tutoring	_____	Soviet

First Viewing: Listening for General Information

activity two

When you watch the first time, try to understand the most important information. After viewing the video, circle the best answer for each of the following questions.

1. The students in this report are studying in:

Brooklyn   Boston   Washington, D.C.

2. Before they begin regular courses, students have to take:

math review   study skills   English as a Second Language

3. Many of these students choose to major in:

biology   pharmacy studies   chemistry

4. The ESL program at Long Island University is:

getting larger   getting smaller   staying the same

Remembering Information

What other information did you understand from the video? As a class, discuss your ideas. Your teacher will write them on the board.

Second Viewing: Listening for Specific Information

Watch the video again. This time, listen for the answers to the following questions. Circle the correct answers.

1. How many students from the former Soviet Union attend college at Long Island University in Brooklyn?

700   600   300

2. Students in this program study English _____ hours per week.

14   16   60

3. How many semesters do most of the students study English?

1–2   3–4   1–3

Third Viewing: Listening for Details

Match the names of the speakers with their descriptions while your teacher plays the video again. Write the letters on the lines. The first one is done for you.

1. Irina Livshets   _C_   a) works in the pharmacy department at Long Island University in Brooklyn.

2. Meryl Perrotta   _____   b) works in the ESL department at the university.

3. Carol Anne Riddell   _____   c) is studying English now.

4. Stanley Zelinski   _____   d) was a pharmacist in Russia.

5. Faina Shenderov   _____   e) is a television news reporter.

Discussing the Video

activity six

With your class or in small groups, discuss the following questions.

1. Students in this program study English sixteen hours per week for one to three semesters before they begin to study other courses. Do you think this is enough? Do you think it is too much? Why?

2. According to this report, many students from the former Soviet Union major in pharmacy studies. Do you have friends with the same major as you? What are the popular fields of study among your friends? Why do you think students from the same country or culture often major in the same field of study?

Writing About School Life

Developing Writing Skills

You read the story of Tan Nguyen and heard about Irina Livshets in the video. Now write a story about your own life in school. Use the information below to help you write your story. (Note: Use the information in the box for ideas. You don't have to answer every question. Also, you may want to write about something in your school life that isn't in the box.)

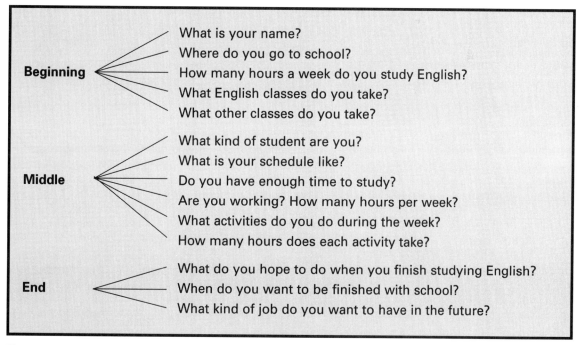

Beginning
- What is your name?
- Where do you go to school?
- How many hours a week do you study English?
- What English classes do you take?
- What other classes do you take?

Middle
- What kind of student are you?
- What is your schedule like?
- Do you have enough time to study?
- Are you working? How many hours per week?
- What activities do you do during the week?
- How many hours does each activity take?

End
- What do you hope to do when you finish studying English?
- When do you want to be finished with school?
- What kind of job do you want to have in the future?

A Step Beyond

1. Arrange a class tour around the school. Your teacher or a guide can show you where all the important services or facilities are.

2. Invite a speaker from a different college or university in your community to talk about the programs and services available on their campus.

Experiencing Nature

in this chapter

You will discuss some different aspects of nature and write a postcard that describes a natural scene. You will watch a short video called "Samson the Bear." It shows what happens when a bear wanders into a neighborhood in southern California. Finally, you will debate an environmental issue: Should some natural wetlands be destroyed to build a new airport runway?

Getting Ready

activity one

Warming Up: Brainstorming

When you read the chapter title "Experiencing Nature," what words and phrases do you think of? Tell them to your teacher as she or he writes them on the board. Are there any words or phrases that you don't understand or find difficult to pronounce? Your teacher will help you understand and pronounce them.

activity two

Discussing Nature

Discuss these questions as a class or in small groups.

1. Do you like to go camping, hiking, or do things away from the city? What kinds of activities do you enjoy? Where do you like to go?

2. Are there any natural areas (mountains, beaches, waterfalls, etc.) that you would like to visit someday? Where are they?

3. What kinds of problems do humans cause for nature?

4. Should countries make laws to protect natural areas like forests? Should they make laws to protect some kinds of animals?

5. What are the most important natural resources in your home country?

Reading About Nature

activity one

Preparing to Read

Look at the four pictures on the next page. What do you see in each one? Discuss what you see with your teacher and your classmates.

Reading

Work with a partner. Read the following paragraphs and match each paragraph to one of the pictures. Write the number of the picture in the box before each paragraph.

> *Listening alternative:* Your teacher will read the paragraphs aloud. As you listen, you will match each one to the appropriate picture.

The World of Nature

A   In some parts of the world, there is a lot of wind all year-round. In these places, people can use windmills like this one to produce electricity. A windmill looks like a huge fan. Using a windmill provides electricity and also saves natural resources like oil and coal.

1.

B   Many different kinds of plants and animals live in this forest. They are both large and small and they need each other to survive. The earth also needs forests like this one for oxygen, but a lot of forest land is disappearing. People don't know if the earth can survive without forest land.

2.

C   This funnel-shaped cloud is called a tornado. It is moving at more than 300 miles per hour. It has already destroyed many homes and buildings. Before it dies out, it will kill at least 20 people. Tornadoes are part of nature too, but they cause a lot of problems.

3.

D   The snow along this mountain road is now more than eight feet high. A lot of snow has been cleared from the road, but some is still there. This kind of road can be very dangerous if you don't have chains on your tires. In about two months, the snow will melt and the road will be safer to drive on.

4.

Understanding the Reading

Exploring Words

R
activity one

Read the words and phrases below. In paragraph A, B, C, or D, on page 13, find a word that has the same meaning. Write the word on the line after the paragraph letter.

Words and Phrases	**Paragraph**	
1. make	A	_produce_
2. moving air	A	_____
3. continue to live	B	_____
4. what animals and people breathe in	B	_____
5. a fast-moving, funnel-shaped cloud	C	_____
6. become liquid	D	_____

Understanding Reference

R W
activity two

Read the following sentence: **In Florida, it is very hot in the summer, but the people there don't mind.** In this sentence, the word **there** refers to the phrase "in Florida." What do the words and phrases below refer to in Paragraphs A–D?

1. In Paragraph A, these places refers to _____.

2. In Paragraph B, they refers to _____.

3. In Paragraph C, it refers to _____.

4. In Paragraph C, they refers to _____.

5. In Paragraph D, there refers to _____.

In each paragraph, find a phrase that refers to something in the picture.

6. Paragraph A: _windmills like this one_ _____

7. Paragraph B: _____

8. Paragraph C: _____

9. Paragraph D: _____

Discussing the Reading

Discuss the answers to the following questions with your class or in small groups.

1. Why do you think the earth's forests are disappearing?

2. Have you ever lived through a tornado or any other kind of "natural disaster?"

3. Why do some areas depend on a heavy snowfall from mountains far away? What will the result be if there isn't enough snow?

activity four

Describing a Picture

Choose one of the pictures below. Work with a partner. Describe the picture, using some of the sentences on the left. Add some of your own words. Write your description on a piece of paper.

It is | sunny.
cloudy.
raining.
snowing.

There is/are | trees.
a lake.
clouds.
a cactus.

You can | swim
ski
hike
sail
climb
picnic | there.

Sharing Your Work

Take turns reading your descriptions to the class. Other students should guess which picture you wrote about.

Then form a group with other students who wrote about the same picture. Share your paragraph with others in the group. Write a new paragraph together that uses the best ideas in the group.

Preparing to Write

Work with a partner. Look at all the nature pictures on pages 13 and 15. Choose one that shows a place you would like to be.

Imagine you are visiting the place in the picture and describe it to your partner. Answer the following questions:

1. Where are you? _____

_____

2. Who is there with you? _____

_____

3. What time of day is it? _____

4. What are you doing? _____

_____

5. What's the weather like? _____

_____

6. How do you feel? Are you afraid, excited, calm? _____

_____

Now listen to your partner's answers to the same questions.

Writing a Postcard

Use your answers to the questions in activity six and write a postcard to a friend. Tell him or her about the place in the picture. Look at the example on page 17.

June 21

JACKSONVILLE FL 32207
PM
23 JUN
1996

Dear Martha,
I am driving through the Mojave Desert
in eastern California. It is almost
8:00 in the evening. I am here with
my family, and we are going to have
dinner now. It is very hot but very
beautiful. I feel happy to be in such
a pretty place.
Hope to see you soon,
Carol

To:

Ms. Martha Rowland

2519 Lee St.

Jacksonville

Florida 32207

Write your postcard in the space below.

Dear _____,

USA
20

Watching a Video
"Samson the Bear"

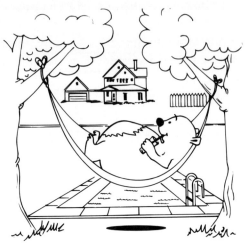

R
activity one

Preparing to Watch

Read the story "Save Our Bear." Think about these questions.

1. Why do some wild animals wander into neighborhoods or near houses?

2. What should people do when wild animals come near their houses?

3. What do you think should happen to Samson?

Save Our Bear

A   The town of Monrovia, California has fallen in love with a bear. They've even given him a name—Samson. Samson is a black bear who has lived all his life in the San Gabriel Mountains. For the past few years, Samson has been wandering into Monrovia neighborhoods looking for food, water and, sometimes, a swimming pool.

B   The California State Fish and Game Commission tried to stop Samson from coming so close to people's houses. They caught him in a bear trap and planned to "put him to sleep." This made the residents of Monrovia angry because they had fallen in love with Samson. They organized a group to save

Samson. This group has written letters to the state and held a news conference to draw attention to Samson's situation. They want Samson to be relocated to a higher area of the mountains or to a zoo. They even say they will pay for Samson's relocation themselves.

C

Relocating Samson might be difficult, however. His teeth are old and worn. The Fish and Game Commission says if they move him higher up in the mountains, he couldn't survive. They also say that zoos already have too many bears and don't want any more.

activity two

Exploring Words

Find these words or phrases in the story. (You will also hear them on the video.) What do you think they mean? Discuss them with your teacher.

put him to sleep   State Fish and Game Commission

residents   survive

relocation   news conference

First Viewing: Listening for General Information

activity three

Read these questions before watching the video. Then answer them during your first viewing of the video segment.

1. Which speaker is the reporter?

A   B   C

2. Which speaker says that Monrovia has "fallen in love with that bear?"

A   B   C

3. Which speaker says that the community will pay for Samson's relocation?

A   B   C

4. Which speakers are speaking at a press conference?

A   B   C

Second Viewing: Listening for Specific Information

Watch the video again. Use these questions to understand some of the details. Read the questions with your teacher before viewing. (Note: Some of the language in the video is difficult. It isn't necessary to understand every word. Listen for the main ideas.)

1. What do you know about Samson?

    age: _____

    weight: _____

    kind of bear: _____

2. Where is Monrovia? (Circle one.)

    a. near San Diego

    b. near the San Gabriel Mountains

    c. near San Francisco

3. When did the Fish and Game Commission capture Samson? (Circle three answers.)

    a. Monday   Saturday   Sunday

    b. morning   afternoon   evening

    c. 9:00   5:00   1:00

4. Who held the news conference? (Circle one.)

    a. Residents and city officials

    b. The Fish and Game Commission

5. Samson was _____. (Circle one.)

    a. put to sleep

    b. held for more observation

    c. set free in the mountains

Third Viewing: Reading and Listening

This time, read the story "Save Our Bear" while you listen. Underline the information in the story as you hear it on the video. Compare your findings with a partner or discuss them with the class.

activity six

Writing About Samson

What do you think happened to Samson? Write a letter to the California State Fish and Game Commission at the address below to find out what happened to Samson. In your letter, tell what you already know about Samson from watching the video and reading the story. Be sure to include your address too. You might get an answer! Write to:

California State Fish and Game Commission
Sacramento, CA 95814
Re: Samson the Bear

```
Your Address
Street
City, State  Zip

Month Day, Year

Director
California State Fish and Game Commission
Sacramento, CA  95814

Re:  Samson the Bear

Dear Director:




















Sincerely,

Your Name
```

Chapter 2 • Experiencing Nature

Conducting a Debate:
The Airport vs. The Wetlands

Learning About Debates

activity one

Talk about these questions with your teacher and your classmates.

1. What is a debate?

2. Have you seen a debate on television in English or in your first language? If so, tell the class about it.

Discussing "Nature" and "Progress"

activity two

In today's society, it often seems that "nature" and "progress" are in conflict with each other. In this activity, you will debate this issue. You and your team will take one side of the issue and try to give the best arguments for your side. The other team will argue against you. Someone (the teacher or other students, for example) will be the judge or "moderator" and decide which team gives the best arguments.

Discuss the following paragraph in groups or as a class:

> Nature is important not only for its beauty but also for the survival of the earth. However, modern life has created many things that destroy plants, animals, and land areas. A lot of people argue about which is more important, saving nature ("the environment"), or the progress of modern life. Have you ever heard any arguments like this? What were they about?

Preparing the Debate

activity three

Look at the two pictures on page 23. What do you see? The airport needs a new runway, but building the runway will destroy a lot of natural life. What do you think should happen?

INTERACTIONS ONE: A Multi-Skills Activity Book

Your teacher will divide the class equally into two groups, a **nature group** and a **progress group.**

1. Each group should read the information below about its own position.

2. Use this information and your own ideas to think of arguments that support your team's position.

3. List the arguments for your position and select one student to present each one.

Group 1: The Progress Group

Your group includes managers of the Southville airport and officials of the city government. The city is growing quickly. The airport has two runways, but that is not enough for the many planes flying in and out of Southville. Planes often have to wait twenty to thirty minutes to take off on the old runway. The people of Southville are angry because the planes are always late. Also, a big company wants to build an office building in Southville that would provide two hundred new jobs. But the company is worried because the airport is too small for the shipping they need to do. The only place for a new runway is on some "wetlands" west of the airport. (Wetlands are like a swamp.) They are controlled by the federal government. You want the federal government to give permission for the wetlands to be drained so that the new runway can be built there.

Group 2: The Nature Group

The members of your group come from the federal government and a Southville environmental group. The city wants to build a runway on some "wetlands" west of the airport. Wetlands are very special lands. There is a lot of water there from the nearby river. Many kinds of plants and animals live in the wetlands that can't live anywhere else. Millions of acres of wet-lands have already been destroyed for houses, office buildings, and shopping malls. The federal government wants to save the wetlands that are left. Also, the water that overflows from the river will flood some parts of the city if the wetlands are destroyed.

Arguments   **Presenter's Name**

_____   _____

_____   _____

_____   _____

_____   _____

_____   _____

_____   _____

_____   _____

_____   _____

activity four

Conducting the Debate

1. Line up your chairs in two rows facing each other, like this:

Group 1

Group 2

2. A speaker from Group 1 presents his or her first argument. (Each argument should be only a few sentences.) Then, for two minutes, anyone from Group 2 can respond to the argument.

3. Repeat the process above for Group 2's first argument.

4. Alternating teams continue until each student has presented one argument with the other team responding.

5. The judge(s) decide(s) who the winning team is.

Writing About the Debate

activity one

Working with Grammar

You are going to write about the debate using several grammar structures. Write sentences or questions about the debate using the cue words in parentheses.

There is/there are:

1. (there/problem/Southville)

There is a problem in Southville.

2. (there/not enough/runways/airport)

_____

3. (there/wetlands/west of the airport)

_____

Impersonal *it*:

4. (it/important/new runway)

It is important to build a new runway.

5. (it/necessary/save the wetlands)

_____

6. (it/possible/both sides/agree?)

_____

Modals *may, can, will,* and *should:*

7. (planes/can't/on time)

_____

8. (Southville/may/lose/new businesses)

_____

9. (many plants and animals/die/without the wetlands)

_____

Present continuous:

10. (government/trying/save the wetlands)

_____

11. (people of Southville/discussing/solution)

_____

Summarizing

> A summary has all the main ideas presented in a reading,
> meeting, debate, etc., but it leaves out most details.
> Summarizing is an important academic skill. You will need
> to summarize what you read and hear in class to answer
> test questions and write papers.

activity two

Use the sentences you wrote in the last activity to summarize the debate.
Discuss the sentences with your teacher. How will you organize them? Will
you give all the points from one side first and then all the points from the
other side? Will you give a point from one side and then a point from the
other and so on? Use some of the following words to organize your sentences into a paragraph.

    because   so   but

Write your summary in the space below and on the next page. Then compare your summaries. Did your classmates organize the sentences in a different way? Do some of those ways seem to work better than others?

_____

_____

_____

_____

_____

_____

_____

_____

_____

_____

_____

_____

_____

_____

_____

activity three

Developing Writing Skills

The newspaper in your area has stories about the runway and the wetlands. Now a lot of people are writing letters to the paper giving their opinions. The part of a newspaper that has people's letters is called the editorial page.

1. Write a letter to the newspaper giving your opinion about the airport runway. Do you think Southville should save the wetlands or build the new runway?

2. Read other students' letters. Who do you agree or disagree with? Discuss this with your class.

3. Create a class editorial page from your letters.

A Step Beyond

1. Learn about an environmental issue in your area by visiting the library, reading the newspaper, watching the local news, or inviting a guest speaker to class.

2. Take a nature hike or a field trip with your class.

3. Watch a video with your class about an environmental issue.

CHAPTER three

Living to Eat or Eating to Live?

in this chapter

Some people "live to eat" and others "eat to live." Which kind of person are you? In this chapter, you will talk about the foods you eat and learn why some foods are more healthy than others. You will also read about the "four basic food groups" and classify some of the foods you eat into these four groups. The video for this chapter gives some important health information about fast food and fat. Finally, a second short reading tells about some American food fads.

Getting Ready

activity one

Warming Up

What are your opinions on food? Write short answers to these questions. Then, discuss your answers with your class or in small groups.

1. What kinds of foods do you think are healthy (good for you)? Do you eat a lot of these? _____

_____

_____

_____

2. Which is more important, for food to be healthy or to taste good? Why?

_____

_____

_____

3. Do you think some people worry too much about whether their food is healthy? Why or why not? _____

_____

_____

activity two

Quick Writing

Choose one of the questions above. Write about it for five to ten minutes. This is a brainstorming activity, so try to write as much as you can without worrying about spelling or grammar.

activity three

Listing Yesterday's Menu

List all the foods or beverages (things to drink) you had <u>yesterday</u>. Write them in the chart on the next page.

Yesterday's Menu		
	Foods	**Beverages**
Breakfast		
Lunch		
Dinner		
Snacks		
Other		

Discussing Your Work

After completing your list, find a partner and compare answers. Which of you ate healthier food? Why do you think so? Share your results with your teacher and the rest of the class.

Reading About Food

Warming Up

Before you read, discuss the following questions with your classmates.

1. Have you heard of the "four basic food groups?" What do you think they are?

2. What types of food do you think make up a "healthy diet?"

3. Which food groups do you think we need to eat the most? The least?

Reading

Read the following passage about the four basic food groups.

The Four Basic Food Groups

During the 1950s, the U.S. Department of Agriculture developed the idea of "four basic food groups." The goal was to help people choose a healthy, balanced diet. The groups include the following:

- Milk and dairy products
- Meat, fish, and poultry
- Fruits and vegetables
- Grains (such as bread and cereal)

There is also a fifth group called "extras." Extras provide extra calories. They include things like sugar, fat, and alcohol. If you choose foods from all four basic groups, and choose the right amounts of each one, some experts say that you will have a healthy diet.

Milk and Dairy Products   The milk group includes all kinds of dairy products: milk, cheese, ice cream, and yogurt. They provide protein, carbohydrates, fats, vitamins, and minerals. Dairy products give our bodies a lot of calcium, which helps bones to grow and stay strong. Milk also contains Vitamin D. Most adults need two servings of milk (skim milk is best) or dairy products each day, but pregnant women and children need more.

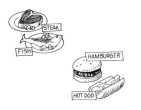

Meats   The meat group includes all meats, poultry, and fish. It also includes beans, peas, and nuts. This group of foods is high in protein, which is important for building body tissues and keeping them healthy. Foods in this group are also high in some vitamins and minerals. You should eat two servings from the meat group each day.

Fruits and Vegetables   Vegetables and fruits provide necessary vitamins, minerals, and carbohydrates. They also provide fiber in your diet. Fiber is good for the digestive system. Fruits and vegetables are also healthy because they don't have much fat in them. Doctors say that adults should have four or more servings of fruits and vegetables each day.

Grains   Grain products such as bread and cereal are composed largely of carbohydrates. They give the body vitamins, minerals, and fiber. The grain group includes all kinds of bread and cereal. It also includes grains like rice or corn. Doctors say that adults should eat four or more servings from the grain group each day.

Water   We don't always think about water as necessary for good health, but it is. In order for the four food groups to work well together, our bodies need plenty of water. Doctors and health experts recommend six glasses per day.

Extras   Most of us eat or drink plenty of extras, such as candy, each day. However, our bodies don't really need them at all. They can also take away our appetite or hunger for the truly healthy foods our bodies need.

Understanding the Reading

activity one

Exploring Words

Which words listed below do you know? Discuss them with your teacher. Then, find each word in the article. How many times do they appear? Circle the words in the article each time you find them.

protein	fiber	carbohydrates
fat(s)	vitamins	digestive system
minerals	servings	calcium

activity two

Discussing the Reading

Discuss these questions with your teacher and classmates.

1. The "four food groups" were developed in the United States during the 1950s. Some people would say they represent a very "American" diet. What do you think?

2. Do people in your culture regularly eat or drink from all four groups?

3. In your experience, is it necessary to eat food from all four groups for good health?

activity three

Using a Chart

Use the information you completed in Yesterday's Menu, activity three on page 31, about the food you ate yesterday. Complete the chart on the next page. Use the reading to put the foods you ate into the basic food groups. Did you eat the recommended number of servings for each group?

Yesterday's Menu			
	What did you have?	**How many servings did you have?**	**How many servings are recommended?**
Milk and Dairy			
Meats			
Fruits and Vegetables			
Grains			
Extras			
Water			

activity four

Discussing Your Diet

Look at your chart. Discuss the following questions with your class.

1. Did you have enough foods from each group?

2. Which groups did you need to get more of? Less of?

3. Overall, was your diet a healthy one yesterday?

Writing About Diets

Exchange books with another student. Look at your partner's list of foods from yesterday. How does the list compare with the foods that doctors and health experts recommend? Write a letter to your partner. In your letter, do the following:

1. Think about his or her diet. Is it a healthy diet? Why or why not? Does the diet have enough foods from each food group?

2. Give your partner some suggestions about his or her diet. What changes does your partner need to make to have a healthier diet?

Example:

> Your diet doesn't have enough fruits and vegetables. I suggest that you eat more servings of those foods.

Watching a Video "Fast Food and Fat"

Preparing to Watch

Before you watch the video, discuss the following questions with your class.

1. What is "fast food?"

2. Do you ever eat fast food? How often?

3. What are your favorite fast-food restaurants?

4. Why do you think fast food is so popular in the U.S.?

5. Do you think fast food is healthy? Why or why not?

Exploring Words

Before viewing the video, discuss the terms below with your teacher and the class. As you watch, notice how these words are used.

healthy   calories

dining   option

cholesterol

First Viewing: Listening for General Information

Read over the following questions before you watch the video for the first time. Then, as you watch the video, check (✔) the correct answers.

1.   What is the name of the book in the report?

_____   *Eat Well in San Diego*

_____   *Healthy Dining in San Diego*

_____   *Low-fat Food in San Diego*

2.   Which people speak during the report?

_____   A news reporter

_____   An employee at El Pollo Loco

_____   A customer at McDonald's

_____   A customer at El Pollo Loco

_____   The regional manager of Jack-in-the-Box

_____   A doctor

_____   A customer at Jack-in-the-Box

3.   Which fast-food restaurants are mentioned?

_____   El Pollo Loco

_____   Wendy's

_____   Burger King

_____   Taco Bell

_____   La Salsa

_____   McDonald's

_____   Jack-in-the-Box

Second Viewing: Listening for Specific Information

Complete the following exercises by circling or checking the answers.

1. The average person needs _____ calories per day.

    2,500   3,000   2,000

2. The average person needs _____ grams of fat per day.

    56   66   86

3. How many restaurants are listed in *Healthy Dining in San Diego?*

    88   98   48

4. Which of these are "danger words" that mean extra fat in the food?

_____ fried	_____ fresh	_____ sauces
_____ broiled	_____ buttery	_____ cheeses
_____ steamed	_____ creamy	_____ boiled

Applying Your Knowledge

Which foods listed below are "high fat" and which are "low fat?" Think about what you learned from the video and fill in the chart.

    taco   milkshakes

    french fries   rice

    beans   flame-broiled chicken

    colossus burger   chicken teriyaki bowl

Low Fat	High Fat

Reading About American Food Fads

activity one

Exploring Words

Before you read, review these words with your teacher.

cholesterol   food additives

red meat   heart disease

cancer

activity two

Skimming for Main Ideas

Before you read the text closely, skim it quickly. Match each paragraph to its main topic. Write the paragraph letter in the blank space. The first one is completed for you.

1. _____   Food additives

2. _____   Fat in your food

3. ___A___   American diets in the 1960s

4. _____   New discoveries that tell us what to eat

5. _____   Low-cholesterol food like bran muffins

activity three

Reading

Read the following passage about "The Great American Diet."

The Great American Diet

A   In the 1960s, scientists discovered cholesterol. Cholesterol, they said, was horrible stuff that entered our arteries and stopped our blood from flowing, resulting in heart attacks. Meat and dairy products contain cholesterol, so people in the United States cut back on red meat and started eating more chicken and fish. McDonald's, Burger King, and Wendy's came out with chicken sandwiches. Most people switched from butter to margarine, and stopped eating eggs for breakfast. If we got our cholesterol levels down, scientists said, we could live longer and stay healthier.

B　　Then a study showed that eating bran muffins lowered cholesterol. Even though many people think that bran muffins taste like cardboard, most fast food restaurants put them on the menu and Americans ate them by the score. All kinds of food items, including those that did not have any cholesterol in them, were labeled "cholesterol free" or "low cholesterol." Americans had their cholesterol checked regularly and compared levels with each other. People said things like, "My cholesterol was 220, but I got it down to 180 by exercise and eating only apples and rice."

C　　In the 1980s, people became worried about "food additives" that caused cancer in rats. These additives are chemicals added to food to make them taste better, look better, or last longer. Food products in grocery stores were labeled "natural" to show that they had no additives. People paid more for "natural" foods than for "unnatural" bread, cereal, and even snack foods like chips and dips.

D　　In the early 1990s, they told us it was "fat that makes you fat." In other words, you could eat all the pasta and potatoes you wanted, as long as you didn't put anything containing fat on them, like butter and sour cream. Then they invented fat-free sour cream and fat-free salad dressings, cookies, tortilla chips, and so on. People munched on fat-free snack foods, expecting to become lean and gorgeous in spite of constant snacking. It didn't happen. Clearly, something other than fat was capable of turning into extra pounds on the human body.

E　　Every day, it seems, there's another scientific discovery that changes the way we eat. The latest discovery is that eating fish, which we were told would reduce cholesterol and prevent heart disease, made no difference in the rate of heart attacks among 4,000 men in a medical study. Scientists are currently saying that olive oil is responsible for the low rate of heart disease among Europeans. Now we have to put olive oil on our fat-free, salt-free, sugar-free, cholesterol-free, additive-free, low-calorie meals. Then we should live forever, right?

Understanding the Reading

activity one

Exploring Words

Can you find words with the following meanings in the reading?

In paragraph A find:

1. a phrase that means <u>released</u>: _____

2. a word that means <u>changed</u>: _____

In paragraph B find:

3. a phrase that means <u>a lot of them</u>: _____

In paragraph C find:

4. a word that means <u>called</u> or <u>named</u>: _____

In paragraph D find:

5. a word that means <u>thin</u>: _____

6. a word that means <u>beautiful</u>: _____

In paragraph E find:

7. a word that means <u>most recent</u>: _____

8. a word that means <u>always</u>: _____

activity two

Understanding Reference

"The Great American Diet" has many words and expressions that refer to (point to) other words in the text. The sentences below are from the reading. Some words in these sentences are <u>underlined</u>. For each underlined word, draw an arrow to the word or phrase that the underlined word refers to. Circle the word or phrase. The first one is done as an example.

1. In the 1960s, scientists discovered cholesterol. Cholesterol, they said, was horrible stuff that entered our arteries and stopped our blood from flowing, resulting in heart attacks.

2. Meat and dairy products contain cholesterol, so people in the United States cut back on <u>their</u> red meat and started eating more chicken and fish.

3. Even though many people think that bran muffins taste like card-
    board, most fast food restaurants put <u>them</u> on the menu and
    Americans ate <u>them</u> by the score.

4. All kinds of food items, even <u>those</u> that did not have any cholesterol
    in them, were labeled "cholesterol free" or "low cholesterol."

5. People said things like, "My cholesterol was 220, but I got <u>it</u> down
    to 180 by exercise and eating only apples and rice."

6. Food products in grocery stores were labeled "natural" to show that
    <u>they</u> had no additives.

7. In other words, you could eat all the pasta and potatoes you wanted,
    as long as you didn't put anything containing fat on <u>them</u>, like but-
    ter and sour cream.

8. People munched on fat-free snack foods, expecting to become lean
    and gorgeous in spite of constant snacking. <u>It</u> didn't happen.

Thinking About the Reading

activity three

Write short answers to each question below. Then discuss them with your
teacher and classmates.

1. Do you know your cholesterol level? If so, is it considered high,
    medium, or low?

2. Have you ever tried to reduce the fat or cholesterol in your diet?
    How?

3. What is the author's attitude (feeling) about people who worry
    about cholesterol and their diets? Find statements in the text to sup-
    port your answer.

4. What is the author's attitude (feeling) about doctors and health
    experts who advise the public? Find statements in the text to sup-
    port your answer.

5. Do you agree with the author's attitude? Why or why not?

activity four

Developing Writing Skills

Write a letter to the regional manager of a fast-food restaurant. In your letter, explain that you are working on a unit about health and food in your ESL class. Ask about the fat content and the number of calories in the restaurant's most popular menu items.

A Step Beyond

R W L S

Take a class field trip to a local fast-food restaurant. Prepare questions in advance about the fat content and number of calories in the restaurant's menu items. When you return to class, write a thank you letter to the restaurant's manager.

_____

_____

_____

_____

_____

_____

_____

_____

_____

_____

_____

CHAPTER **four**

Getting Around the Community

in this chapter

You will talk about your city and community, and read about some cities and communities in different parts of the United States. The video for this chapter shows parts of a community festival in Little Italy in New York City. Next, you will read about a doctor in Miami, Florida, who works with the poor and homeless, and discuss some organizations that help people solve problems in communities in other parts of the United States. Finally, you will write a letter to a community organization to find out more information about what it does.

45

Getting Ready

Warming Up

Discuss the following questions with your class or in small groups.

1. What do you like best about the community you live in?

2. Are there activities in your community where people work together to make the community better? Do they do volunteer work or organize to help other people?

3. Does your community have any special celebrations, parties, or meetings?

Reading About Communities in the United States

Exploring Words

activity one

What is your community like? Review the words and phrases in the questions below with your teacher. Then discuss the questions with your class or in small groups. Some questions may have more than one answer.

1. Is your community

—a big city?

—a large town?

—a college town?

—a small town?

—a suburb of a city?

—rural (in the country)?

2. Is your community

—industrial?

—agricultural?

—a vacation resort area?

—mostly business offices?

—mostly residential (homes)?

3. Are most of the people in your community

—natives of the area?

—people who moved there from somewhere else?

4. Does your community include tourists

—in certain seasons?

—all year-round?

—almost never?

5. Are the stores in your community

—all located downtown?

—mostly in shopping malls?

—individual buildings far apart?

6. Are the buildings in your community

—tall skyscrapers?

—low houses, stores, and schools?

—modern (made of glass and steel)?

—historic?

7. Are the houses

—close together with small yards in the back only?

—far apart with big yards?

activity two

Preparing to Read

Look at the four pictures on the next two pages. What do you see in each one? Discuss the pictures with your teacher and classmates.

activity three

Reading

Work with a partner. Read the four paragraphs on pages 48 and 49. Match each paragraph to one of the pictures. Write the number of the picture in the box before each paragraph.

Listening alternative: Your teacher will read the paragraphs aloud. As you listen, you will match each one to the appropriate picture.

Communities in the United States

A   Roger and Kathleen are brother and sister. They are both students at a university. Their parents live in another state, but Roger and Kathleen often go home on a Sunday for a big family dinner. It's easy: All they have to do is drive across the river! It's very hot and muggy in the summer, but the family has a summer home up in the mountains where it's cooler and drier. When Roger and Kathleen are at school, they live in high-rise dormitories with a lot of other students. They like to go downtown on Saturday night and listen to jazz or the blues.

1. **New York City, New York**

B   Marco Andre drives to work every morning. It takes him almost an hour because the traffic is usually terrible! He hates the traffic, but he sees a lot of advantages to living where he does. The weather is very good. It's warm and sunny most of the year. Marco likes to go to the beach on weekends with his friends and swim in the big ocean waves. Sometimes they hike in the mountains instead, or ski there in the winter when there's snow. Marco likes to be outside whenever he can, and he lives in a place where he can be outside most of the year!

2. **Memphis, Tennessee**

C   Helena Richards and her son, Mike, like to be outside, too, but when they're outside, they're working. Mike is only ten years old, but he gets up at dawn to feed the chickens and check on the baby pigs before he gets on the bus to go to school. He loves taking care of the animals. When he gets home, he rides his horse around their big farm and watches the farm workers driving the huge combine tractors. His mother discusses the day's work with the two men who work for her, and then they milk the cows.

3. **Ames, Iowa**

D Bert and Angela Sims live in an apartment on the twelfth floor of a tall building. Every morning, they take the subway to work. Angela doesn't like the crowds on the subway, but it's easier than driving in the traffic and finding a parking space. On the way home, either Angela or Bert stops to buy something for dinner that night. In the winter, it's a cold walk from the subway station to their apartment. On those days, Bert thinks about moving to a warmer climate. He and Angela both like having theaters, museums, and restaurants close by, however, so they will probably stay where they are.

4. Los Angeles, California

Understanding the Reading

Classifying and Listing Information

R
activity one

List some of the things these people like about their communities. One has been completed for you.

Roger & Kathleen	Marco Andre	The Richards	The Sims
_____	_____	_____	theater
_____	_____	_____	_____
_____	_____	_____	_____

Exploring Words

R
activity two

Read the words and phrases below. In paragraphs A, B, C, or D on pages 48 and 49, find a word or phrase that has the same meaning. Write the word or phrase in the line after the paragraph letter.

Words and Phrases		Paragraph	
1.	humid; a lot of moisture in the air	A	muggy
2.	tall, with many floors	A	_____
3.	walk for fun, usually in the country	B	_____
4.	good aspects, benefits	B	_____
5.	very early in the morning	C	_____
6.	look to see if things are OK	C	_____
7.	large group	D	_____
8.	near	D	_____

INTERACTIONS ONE: A Multi-Skills Activity Book

Discussing the Reading

Discuss these questions with your classmates. Be prepared to use the information from the paragraphs on pages 48 and 49 to explain your answers.

1. Would Bert and Angela be happy living in Ames, Iowa? Why or why not?

2. Would Roger and Kathleen be happy in New York? Why or why not?

3. Which community is most like your community? Why?

4. Which community is least like your community? Why?

Writing About Communities

Reread the paragraphs about communities in the United States. Which of these communities would you like to live in? Why? If you don't want to live in any of the communities, what type would you want to live in? Write a paragraph about the type of community that you like best.

Watching a Video "A Cultural Celebration"

Preparing to Watch

You are going to watch a video of the St. Anthony's Festival. It takes place in Little Italy, New York City. It's called Little Italy because people from Italy settled there many years ago. Their children and their children's children stayed there. Today, many of the people in the community have ancestors from Italy.

In your home country, do some cities have special communities, with people from specific ethnic, cultural, or religious groups?

activity two

First Viewing: Listening for General Information

During the video, listen and watch for the answers to these questions. Discuss the answers with your class after you watch the video for the first time.

1. Is the St. Anthony's Festival only for people who have ancestors from Italy?

2. What is the reporter trying to do?

3. Name three things people are doing at the festival.

Second Viewing: Listening for Details

activity three

Listen again. Match the speakers with the words they say. Write the letters on the lines.

Speakers	**What they said**
1. Man in white T-shirt _____	a) Pretty good.
2. Joe from Ozone Park _____	b) Very good. What? Drink piña colada.
3. Woman with dark hair _____	c) We got piña coladas, strawberry daiquiris, wine, beer, everything.
4. White-haired woman _____	d) Whaddya wanna know? *(What do you want to know?)*

Third Viewing: Reading and Listening

activity four

Look at the pairs of words and phrases below. You will hear only *one* of each pair in the video. Circle the word or phrase you hear.

1. games of chance   games of choice

2. baseball twos   baseball toss

3. thirty-first   forty-fourth

4. Canal to Grant   Camel to Branch

5. She's a shy one.   She's the show one.

Role Play

Work in pairs. One student will take the part of Joe from Ozone Park. The other student will be the news reporter. The reporter should interview Joe. Ask the following questions, then add a few of your own questions. Your teacher may ask you to act out the role play for the class.

1. What are you doing at the festival?

2. What kinds of people do you see at the festival?

3. Do you like working at the festival?

4. Your own question: _____

5. Your own question: _____

Learning About Communities

Community Role Play

Work in groups of three or four. Each student chooses a different picture below. Then take turns being "in the spotlight." When you are "in the spotlight," the other students can ask you questions. You must answer like the person in the picture.

Examples:

- What is your name?
- How old are you?
- Where are you from?
- Could you tell us about your family?
- How did you learn to _____?
- Tell us about your job.

Developing Writing Skills

activity two

Write a paragraph describing yourself as the person you choose on page 53. Explain what you do in the community. Be sure to use "I." For example:

My name is _____. I am a mail carrier. I deliver mail to people in the community. Sometimes I walk; sometimes I drive a truck.

Reading About Communities

Exploring Words

activity one

Discuss the following words with your teacher before you read the passage below.

clinic   heroic   addicts   lungs   volunteer

Reading

activity two

Read the following passage about a "local hero."

A "Local Hero" in Miami

A   Many people do volunteer work in their communities, which makes them "heroes" to the people they help. One of these people is Dr. Pedro José Greer, a doctor from Miami. Dr. Greer runs a medical clinic in a shelter for homeless people. He works in the clinic three days a week. He has gotten other doctors to volunteer their time in the clinic too. Dr. Greer doesn't just work in the clinic, he also goes out into the community to tell people how the clinic can help them.

B   Dr. Greer started the clinic because homeless people, drug addicts, and the poor in Miami were dying. They had diseases like tuberculosis, a disease of the lungs. They had no money to see doctors and get treatment. Now they can come to Dr. Greer's clinic, the Camillus Health Concern, to get medical care.

C   Dr. Greer's parents came to Miami from Cuba. He was born in Miami and went to school there. He always knew that he wanted to take care of the poor and homeless. He has won several awards for his work, but he doesn't think that he does anything heroic. He enjoys working with the poor and homeless and loves his community.

Understanding the Reading

Talking About Heroes

Discuss the following questions with the class or in small groups.

1. What do you think a "hero" is?

2. Try to think of three names of famous people for each of the following groups.

Sports heroes: _____

_____

Military heroes (past or present): _____

_____

Adventure heroes (explorers, astronauts, etc.): _____

_____

3. What kinds of work do you think "local heroes" do?

Solving Community Problems

Reading a Directory

activity one

Sometimes the best solution for community problems is for people to work together. Even one person, like Dr. Greer, can make a difference. Page 56 is a page from a directory. It lists some community programs run by individuals, churches, and charitable organizations that are helping to solve problems in U.S. communities. As you read, think about the questions below. After looking over the list, answer these questions with a partner.

1. Which organization works to help the environment?

2. Which organization helps people to deal with death?

3. Which organization helps homeless people to find jobs?

4. How would you choose to help people in your community?

Organization and Address	Services
National 4-H Council (Find your local branch by looking in your local phone book under county government, Cooperative Extension Office.)	Offers educational programs for young people about the environment, the workplace, fighting violence, and helping the community.
Chattanooga Venture Contact: Susan Tillman 506 Broad Street Chattanooga, TN 37402	Organizes projects to improve the community including: • restoring historic buildings such as Tivoli Theater • setting up the Family Violence Shelter for abused women and children • forming neighborhood associations to fight crime
New Community Corporation Contact: Rona Parker Director of Public Affairs 233 West Market Street Newark, NJ 07103	Sets up projects to restore the central district of the city, including: • building a shopping center • building low-cost housing • operating day-care centers for children • providing a nursing home for the elderly
Code: Blue Contact: Captain Randy Ely Fort Worth Police Department 1000 Throckmorton Fort Worth, TX 76102	Helps to reduce crime in Fort Worth by: • organizing citizens to take law enforcement training and patrol the streets • working with community groups to understand problems that lead to crime
Zen Hospice Project 273 Page Street San Francisco, CA 94102	Runs programs for people who are dying, including: • operating a hospice (place for dying people to stay) • training volunteers to work in the hospice and other hospices in San Francisco • providing educational speakers on dealing with disease and death
The Green Plant Center Resource Renewal Institute Fort Mason Center, Building A San Francisco, CA 94123	Provides information and educational services about the environment.
Alpha Project Contact: Bob McElroy, Executive Director 299 17th Street San Diego, CA 92101	Helps homeless people in San Diego find jobs and offers them counseling, legal, and medical services.

Writing a Letter of Request

Work with a partner. Choose one of the organizations in the chart, or find a community organization where you live. Write a letter to request more information about the organization and what it does. Follow the letter format below.

```
Your Address
Street
City, State   Zip Code


Month, Day, Year


Name of Community Organization
Street
City, State   Zip Code


Dear _____:


Tell the reader of the letter:


• Who you are and why you are contacting them
• What you want to know about the organization
• What you wish to receive from them (for example,
  news clippings or brochures)


Don't forget to thank the organization in advance for
their help.


Sincerely,


Signature


Your Name Typed
```

Following Up

If you receive an answer to your letter, summarize the information you get for the class. Tell what the organization does and show any pictures they send you.

Predicting the Future of Your Community

Predicting

What do you think is going to happen to your community in the future? Do you like change or do you want everything to stay the same? Write one sentence about each of the subjects below. Write what you think is going to happen in your community.

For example:

I think my city is going to build a subway or commuter train. Tourism might increase when the new stadium is open.

a. transportation

b. jobs

c. education

d. housing

e. crime

f. traffic

g. shopping

h. entertainment

activity two

Discussing Your Predictions

Work with two or three other students. Compare your sentences. Do you agree on what is going to happen in the future? Each group should choose three sentences that they wrote together, and choose one person to write them on the chalkboard. Your teacher may check your sentences before you put them on the chalkboard. Read the predictions of the other groups. Do you agree? Your teacher may ask you to explain your predictions.

activity three

Writing About Predictions

Choose one of the predictions from the class discussions. Think about the following questions:

1. What is going to happen?

2. How is it going to happen?

3. Who is going to make it happen?

4. Will the results be good or bad?

5. How will people feel about the change?

6. How will people's lives be better (or worse) because of the change?

7. If you think the change is bad, what do you think people can or should do to stop it?

Write about your prediction. Imagine that you are writing for the local newspaper. Explain your prediction to the people in the community. What do you think they want to know about the future?

Read your prediction to the class (or share it with them on the computer). Whose predictions do you think will come true?

A Step Beyond

Put together a class newspaper with all of the predictions your class made. Distribute the newspaper to other classes. Discuss your predictions or take a school poll to see how many students agree with the predictions.

CHAPTER **five**

Home

You will talk and read about different types of housing, and think about some reasons that people have for buying or renting a house or apartment. The video segment tells about a program that helps buyers get loans for down payments to purchase a house. You will also read two advertisements and compare and contrast the features of two different apartment communities. Finally, you will describe your dream house or apartment.

Getting Ready

activity one

Warming Up

Answer these questions with your class or in small groups.

1. Are you living in an apartment, condo, dormitory, or house? How do you like it?

2. If you could improve the place where you live, what would you do?

3. Do you think it's better to rent or buy? Why?

4. Nowadays, do you think it's easy for families to find a good place to live?

activity two

Quick Writing

Choose one of the questions above. Write about it for five minutes. Try to write as much as you can without worrying about grammar or spelling.

Reading About Buying a House

activity one

Preparing to Read

Discuss the answers to these questions with your class or in small groups.

1. In the United States, many people believe that you save money if you buy a house rather than pay rent. What do you think?

2. Is this true in other countries?

3. If you could buy a house, what kind would it be?

activity two

Exploring Words

Discuss these terms with your teacher before you read:

real estate agent	investment	interest (on a loan)
income taxes	price range	mortgage loan
take home pay	condominium	

INTERACTIONS ONE: A Multi-Skills Activity Book

Reading

Read the following story about buying a house.

House for Sale?

A I really liked my apartment. It was big, with high ceilings, and the building had a swimming pool and tennis courts. But my friends said I should buy a house. If I bought a house, then I could take the interest on the mortgage loan off my income taxes. Also, a house is an investment. Houses almost always increase in value; so, when I sell it, I'll get more money than I paid for it.

B So I started looking for a house. First, I looked in the Sunday newspaper under "Houses for Sale." All the houses sounded good in the ads. How was I going to decide? I figured out what price I could afford to pay. The experts say to spend about two and a half times your annual salary, or to make monthly payments equal to about 28% of your take-home pay. Next, I decided what part of the city I wanted to live in. Then, I looked in that area in my price range.

C I called the real estate agent for one house, but she told me it was too expensive. Then she took me to see other houses. I looked at traditional ranch houses (small rooms, low ceilings, one floor with a garage), contemporary houses (high ceilings, open spaces, high heating bills), zero lots (houses right next to each other with no lawns and no privacy), condominiums (the same thing as apartments, but you own them and have to pay for repairs), and cottages (small houses, low ceilings, no garage). It was so confusing!

D Finally, one night when I was ready to give up, the real estate agent took me to a house that I decided to buy immediately. It was a traditional ranch house but the bedrooms were large, the den had a wonderful fireplace, and the fenced yard was lovely and private. Now, I have a comfortable, attractive house and no money to buy furniture to put in it!

Understanding the Reading

Matching

The author looked at five different kinds of houses:

a. traditional ranch house   **d.** cottage

b. contemporary house   **e.** condominium.

c. zero lot

Write the letters in the boxes to match the kinds of houses with the pictures.

1.

2.

3.

4.

5.

Discussing the Reading

Discuss these questions with your class or in small groups.

1. What two things did the author of this story have to decide before buying a house? Underline the two sentences in paragraph B that show what the author did.

2. What kind of home did the author finally buy? Underline all the specific details about her new home in Paragraph D.

3. Do you like the home she bought? If you could choose one of the styles she looked at, which one would you choose?

4. According to the author's friends, you can save money if you buy a house. Do you think they are right?

Working with Grammar: Verbs and Transition Words

Find all the examples of past tense verbs in *House for Sale?* Next, find examples of other verbs that are not in the past tense. What's the difference between the two groups? What do the sentences with past tense verbs tell you? What do the sentences with the other types of verbs tell you?

Transition Words (1)

Transition words show relationships between sentences or ideas. Some common transition words are: *but, also, then, or, next, now, first, finally.* Here are some types of relationships:

Type of Relationship	Shows you that
additional	something is being added
choice	there is more than one choice
contrasting	two things that conflict are being discussed
time	one event comes after another

The transition words below are from the reading. What kind of relationship does each transition word show? Find each word in the reading and write the relationship on the lines. The first one is done for you.

Transition Words		Relationship
Paragraph A:	but	_contrasting_
	also	_____
	then	_____
Paragraph B:	first	_____
	or	_____
	next	_____
	then	_____
Paragraph C:	but	_____
	then	_____
Paragraph D:	finally	_____
	now	_____

Writing About Homes

How did you find your present home? Was your experience similar to or different from the author's in *House for Sale?* Talk about the questions below with a partner. Then, write your own short essay about how you found your present home (house, condo, or apartment).

1. What things were most important to you (price range, location, size, style or architecture, number of bedrooms/baths, or yard)?

2. What kinds of places did you look at?

3. Did anyone help you? How did you get information about where to look?

4. How did you choose your home? What things about your home did you like?

5. Did you make a good decision? Do you enjoy living there?

Watching a Video
"Buying a Home"

Exploring Words

R
activity one

Before viewing the video, go over the following terms with your teacher.

mortgage payment   default (on a loan)

home equity   first-time buyer

down payment   collateral

finance (a loan)   closing costs

qualified (to buy a home)

activity two

Preparing to Watch

Talk about the following questions with your class or in small groups before you watch the video. Compare your answers to those given in the video.

1. How long are most mortgage loans in the U.S.?

2. What percentage of the price is the usual down payment on a house?

3. How do first-time home buyers get the money for a down payment?

First Viewing: Listening for General Information

activity three

Read these questions before watching the video. After viewing, circle the best answer for each question.

1. Circle all the speakers that appear in the video segment:

a news reporter   a real estate agent

a home buyer   a mortgage company employee

2. This news report is about a program called:

Zero Down   Generation Link   Happy House Hunting

3. This report is about buying a house in:

Arizona   Florida   California

Second Viewing: Listening for Specific Information

activity four

Circle the correct answer for the following questions.

1. In Generation Link, the buyer needs _____ to sign in order to get the loan.

a sponsor   a parent   a relative

2. The down payment in Generation Link is _____.

10%   5%   0%

3. The sponsor can pledge part of their _____.

home   home equity   furniture

4. Loans in this program can be as low as

$10,000 $20,000 $30,000

or as high as

$53,000 $103,000 $203,000

Fill in the answers to these questions.

5. Who pays the closing costs in Generation Link?

_____

6. The sponsor's collateral is released after the buyer makes payment for _____ years.

Discussing the Video

Discuss the following questions with your class or in small groups.

1. Have you ever tried to save money for a down payment? Did you succeed? If not, how would you go about saving that much money?

2. This report was about buying a house in California. Houses there are more expensive than in most other places in the U.S. Why do you think that is?

3. Do you think that the cost of housing makes California a bad place to live? How high are home prices where you live?

Drawing a Floor Plan

Exploring Words

Review the following words with your teacher and classmates:

living room	bathroom
dining room	closet
kitchen	walk-in closet
family room	laundry room
TV room	entrance hall
den or study	front door
hall	back door
porch	floor(s)
basement	storage room
bedroom	attic

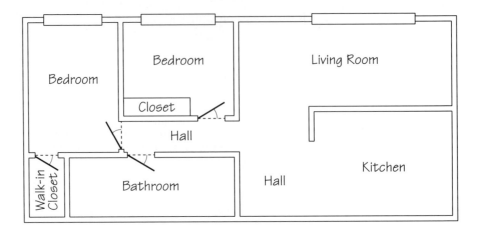

Understanding Instructions

activity two

The drawing above is a floor plan of an apartment. In the box below, you are going to draw another floor plan, that of your teacher's house or apartment. In order to draw it, you will need to ask your teacher a lot of questions. Use a pencil because you may need to erase something! The following words and expressions will help you to ask the questions.

"Where is the . . . ?"

"Is there a . . .?"

"How many . . . does your house (apartment) have?"

"How big is the . . .?"

"What's next to the . . . ?"

Floor plan of your teacher's house

INTERACTIONS ONE: A Multi-Skills Activity Book

Understanding Apartment Ads

activity one

Reading

One of the ways people often find a place a place to live is by reading apartment "ads" (short word for "advertisements"). Read the two apartment ads here and on the next page. Work with a partner or in groups of three or four students to compare and contrast the ads. What is similar? What is different? Write down your answers. Your teacher may ask you to read them to the class.

VALLEY VILLAGE

IF LOCATION AND VALUE ARE WHAT YOU'RE SEARCHING FOR, THEN LOOK NO FURTHER THAN VALLEY VILLAGE! This small, quiet, garden community is centrally located in Ranch Valley, just minutes away from shopping, beaches, and downtown. Ranch Valley is a great residential neighborhood with malls, movie theaters, restaurants, and parks nearby. Valley Village is the best housing value in the area, with spacious floor plans, fully-equipped kitchens, and central air conditioning—all at a very low price. But don't take our word for it, come by today and discover for yourself the excellent value at Valley Village!

1BDR/1 BTH from $585   2BDR/2 BTH from $685

FEATURES: Pool, spa, and BBQ grill. Apartments feature wall-to-wall carpet, draperies, vertical/mini-blinds, and **central A/C/heat.** Foyer closet, separate dining room. Large, fully-equipped, electric kitchen and **frost-free** refrigerator, **self-cleaning** oven, pantry, double sink, disposal, and dishwasher. Bedrooms with separate vanity and dressing area. Spacious linen, walk-in and wall-to-wall closets. Sliding glass door leads to private patio/balcony and outside storage. Reserved parking, laundry facilities. Furnished units available. **Small pets OK** with approval.

Valley Village

VENICE COURTS

WELOME TO THE NEIGHBORHOOD . . . the perfect environment for peaceful living. A uniquely planned and designed community with an Italian flair offers you the best in amenities and **custom** features . . . with the kind of quality you expect in your **home**. The open air feeling of spacious **sunny** apartments, panoramic **views**, and rolling terrain distinguishes Venice Courts.

2BDR/2 BTH from $740   3BDR/3 BTH from $840
$600 MOVE-IN PACKAGE
Limited time offer. Call for details.

FEATURES: outdoor pool, spa, barbecues, playground. Clubhouse w/fireside lounge, TV, billiards, kitchen. Interiors feature ceramic tile foyers, fireplaces, cathedral ceilings, plant shelves. Mini/vertical blinds, ceiling fans, central air, gas heat, upgraded plumbing and lighting fixtures, large patio/balcony w/storage. Efficient kitchens include tiled counters, many cabinets, pantry, complete Whirlpool appliance package w/microwave. Full-size washer/gas dryer hook-ups and laundry facilities. Spacious baths w/marble vanities. Abundance of storage space throughout including walk-in closets, shelves, linens. Private garages available. Cable ready. No pets.

activity two

Comparing Advertisements

In small groups, discuss the features listed in the chart below. Make notes about each apartment complex on the chart (sometimes you only need to write "yes" or "no"). When you finish discussing the chart, decide which apartment you would rather live in. Discuss your reasons with your group and then with the whole class. Which apartment complex does the class like?

Features	Valley Village	Venice Courts
distance from shopping, theater, etc.	_____	_____
number of bedrooms	_____	_____
rent	_____	_____
pool	_____	_____
playground	_____	_____
garage	_____	_____
microwave	_____	_____
high ceilings	_____	_____
ceiling fans	_____	_____
clubhouse	_____	_____
central air	_____	_____
laundry hook-ups	_____	_____
cable TV	_____	_____
patio/balcony	_____	_____
storage area	_____	_____
dishwasher	_____	_____
pets O.K.?	_____	_____

Describing Your Dream House or Apartment

activity one

Describing and Drawing

You are going to describe your dream house or apartment to a partner.

1. Work in pairs.

2. **Student One** describes his or her dream house to **Student Two.** **Student Two** should ask **Student One** the questions below. Both students should take notes because later you will draw your partner's dream house!

     a. How many rooms are there?
     b. Where is each room?
     c. What kind of furniture is in each room?
     d. What is special about this house?

3. Here are some words and expressions you might want to use:

The furniture is:	*The house/apartment is made of:*
modern	wood
antique	bricks
rustic (country-style)	cement block
of an era (1950s, 1960s, etc.)	stucco
The house/apartment has:	*The kitchen has:*
a swimming pool	modern appliances
a tennis court	a breakfast area
a fireplace	a breakfast counter
two stories	a built-in stove and dish-
washer	
a basement	a microwave

4. After **Student One** has finished, reverse roles. **Student Two** describes his/her dream house to **Student One.**

5. After both students have described their dream houses, each tries to draw at least one aspect of the other student's dream house on a separate sheet of paper.

Writing a Letter

Choose one of the following:

1. Write a letter to a local real estate agent. Describe the kind of house you want. Ask how much money you would need in order to purchase a house, and how much your monthly payments would be.

2. Write a letter to a local apartment management company about the kind of apartment you would like to live in. Describe the features you want and tell how much you are willing to pay. (Use the ads for Valley Village and Venice Courts to help you identify the features you want.)

A Step Beyond

1. Look for real estate booklets with apartment advertisements in local grocery stores or banks. Choose an apartment you would like to live in. What do you like about it? Compare your choice with other students.

2. Invite an apartment rental agent or local real estate agent to talk to the class. Ask the rental agent to talk about laws concerning the rights and responsibilities of landlords and renters in your state. Ask the real estate agent to talk about how to choose a property to buy and how to arrange for a mortgage.

CHAPTER six

Emergencies and Strange Experiences

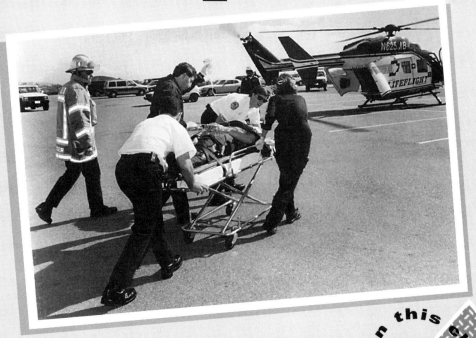

in this chapter

You will read and discuss different kinds of natural disasters and emergency situations, and look at safety rules for dealing with different emergencies. The video segment tells about a recent terrible earthquake in Japan. Finally, you will role play some emergency situations and choose an emergency situation to write about.

Getting Ready

activity one

Warming Up

In this chapter, you will look at several different kinds of emergencies. One type of emergency is a natural disaster. Natural disasters include bad storms, earthquakes, and other things that occur in nature. Discuss the following questions with your class or in small groups.

1. What kinds of storms or other natural disasters happen in places where you have lived?

2. What natural disasters do you remember reading or hearing about in other parts of the world?

3. What kinds of disasters do you think cause the most damage?

Reading About Natural Disasters

activity two

Jigsaw Reading

Work in groups to do the following reading activity.

1. The class should divide into five groups.

2. Each group should read one of the following passages about natural disasters. One person in the group should take notes about important points.

3. Discuss your topic with your group and your teacher. Be sure you understand it and can talk about it with other students.

4. When you are ready, find a partner from another group. Everyone in the class should do this at the same time.

5. Explain the information about your topic to your partner. Then, your partner should explain his or her information to you.

6. When you finish, find another partner from another group and exchange information again.

7. Continue until you have information on all the disasters.

Tornadoes

Tornadoes are long, funnel-shaped clouds of air that whirl around at speeds of more than 300 miles per hour. They usually occur in hot, humid (moist) weather in late spring or summer. Hot air rises from the ground. Cooler air above meets the hot air and causes the air to turn around faster and faster. A tornado may reach from the clouds to the ground and may strike the ground several times before it disappears. Tornadoes usually travel along a path from ten to fifty miles long. They may pick things up from the ground and move them hundreds of meters. Most tornadoes occur in the midwestern part of the United States, in Australia, and in Russia.

Winter Storms

Three types of winter storms can be hazardous.

1. *Blizzard.* This is the most dangerous winter storm. A storm is called a blizzard when there is heavy snow and winds of 35 miles per hour or more, and the temperature is below 20 degrees Fahrenheit (7 degrees Celsius). Often the wind blows the snow around so that it is almost impossible to see. Walking is dangerous because you can easily become lost.
2. *Snowstorm.* In a heavy snowstorm, there may be four inches of snow or more in twelve hours. Driving is dangerous because of slippery or blocked roads and because it may be hard to see where you are going.
3. *Ice Storm.* This storm occurs when the temperature is around 28 to 32 degrees Fahrenheit and it is raining. The rain freezes into ice on the roads, ground, and trees. Tree branches may break off because the ice makes them very heavy. The branches can fall on power lines and cut off the electric power. Driving is extremely hazardous until the roads are clear, because the ice is thick and slippery.

Earthquakes

An earthquake happens when the surface or crust of the earth begins to shake suddenly and violently. Very large plates make up the earth's crust. Pressure on these plates comes from below the earth's surface. The pressure builds up over many years and eventually may cause the plates of the crust to move, creating an earthquake.

Not all earthquakes cause damage and injury. Most are very mild. About 15,000 earthquakes occur each year, but only about one hundred are very destructive. Every part of the world has earthquakes, but in most places they are not strong. For example, in the northeastern part of the United States there are few strong earthquakes. If you mark on a world map the places where earthquakes often occur, your marks will form two large belts, the Pacific belt and the Mediterranean belt.

Hurricanes

A hurricane is a very strong storm. It begins in tropical areas, with gentle winds over the ocean. These winds can become strong and develop into tropical storms. If they become even stronger than tropical storms, they are called hurricanes. A hurricane's winds are faster than 73 miles per hour. In many cases, the winds are faster than 100 miles per hour. Usually a hurricane covers a very large area and brings with it thunder, lightning, and a lot of heavy rain. Hurricanes start mainly in the West Indies and the Gulf of Mexico. They

also occur in the Pacific, where they are called typhoons.

Hurricanes have "eyes." The eye of the hurricane is the center of the storm. When the eye passes over, it feels as if the storm is over because the wind stops blowing. But the storm is really only half over.

Until recently, all hurricanes had women's names. Now, however, half of the hurricanes have men's names and half have women's names.

INTERACTIONS ONE: A Multi-Skills Activity Book

Floods

Rivers are important and beautiful parts of nature, but sometimes a river becomes so full of water that it rises over its banks, causing a flood. Rivers usually flood in the spring. That's because the snow melts, and produces a lot of water. Also, spring rains frequently add to the water from the melting snow. These two actions together may produce more water than the river can hold. Then, water overflows the banks of the river.

Heavy rainstorms can also cause floods. For example, when a hurricane moves in from the sea, it sometimes brings water faster than the rivers can carry it away. If this happens, the rivers will flood. A short heavy rainstorm can cause a flood if the ground is already full of water or if it is too dry. When the ground is very dry, it cannot absorb much water quickly.

Talking About Emergencies

R L S
activity one

Matching

You are going to decide what to do when a natural disaster occurs. The list of safety rules on the right side of the page are recommendations from the U.S. Department of Civil Defense. Match the rules with the natural disasters on the left side of the page. Write the letters of the rules in the blanks. There will be three rules for each disaster. When you finish, discuss your answers with the class.

1. floods

_____

_____

_____

2. earthquakes

_____

_____

_____

3. tornadoes

_____

_____

_____

4. hurricanes

_____

_____

_____

5. snowstorms

_____

_____

_____

a. Go to the basement or a small windowless hall or bathroom.

b. Avoid low areas.

c. Leave low-lying beach areas.

d. Do not enter or leave a building.

e. Leave your car if it stalls (stops running).

f. If you are outside, lie flat in a ditch or low place.

g. Do not cross a stream.

h. Sit or stand in an inside doorway.

i. Drive at a 90-degree angle to the threat (disaster).

j. Cover up the windows with boards.

k. Stay in the car if you are stranded (left in a helpless situation).

l. Don't go out during the calm period in the middle of the storm.

m. Do not use wood-burning stoves or kerosene heaters indoors without enough ventilation.

n. If you are outdoors, stay away from overhead electric wires, poles, or anything else that might shake loose or fall.

o. Make sure you have chains or special tires on your car.

Using Transition Words

Transition Words (2)

As you learned in Chapter Five, certain words in sentences and paragraphs show the relationship of one sentence or part of a sentence to the next. For example, look at the first sentence from the selection about floods:

> Rivers are important and beautiful parts of nature, *but* sometimes a river becomes so full of water that it rises over its banks, causing a flood.

The sentence tells two things about rivers:

GOOD: Rivers are important and beautiful.

BAD: Sometimes rivers flood.

This is a contrast of good and bad. The word *but* shows a contrast. Transition words often tell the reader that the writer is about to give:

  a. **Additional (more) information on the same subject**
     Transition words: *and, also, furthermore*

  b. **An explanation or example of a word or phrase**
     Transition words: *for example, for instance*

  c. **The next action**
     Transition words: *next, second, then, finally*

  d. **The cause or result of something**
     Transition words: *because, therefore, so*

  e. **Some opposite or contrasting information**
     Transition words: *but, however, yet*

activity two

Look at the reading passage about floods. Find transition words with the following meanings. Write the sentences below.

1. Cause or result: _____

2. Addition: _____

3. Next action: _____

4. Example: _____

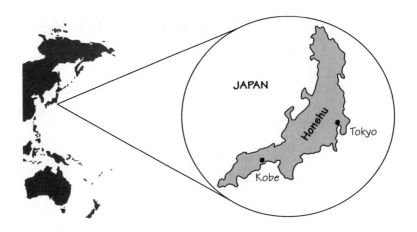

Watching a Video
"An Earthquake in Japan"

Preparing to Watch

activity one

Discuss the following questions with your class or in small groups before
you watch the video.

1. Have you ever experienced an earthquake?

2. Where do you think most earthquakes happen?

3. Would you live in a place that had frequent earthquakes, snowstorms, hurricanes, or tornadoes? Why or why not?

Exploring Words

activity two

Before watching the video, discuss the terms below with your teacher and
the class. As you watch, notice how these words and phrases are used.

ruins

devastating

destruction

aftershocks

allay one's fears

activity three

First Viewing: Listening for General Information

Read these questions and try to answer them after your first viewing of the video segment.

1. Where is the reporter?

2. Where did the earthquake take place?

3. How many passengers does the reporter interview?

4. Which passenger says that this was the biggest earthquake in eighty years, the pilot or the young man?

activity four

Second Viewing: Listening for Specific Information

We often get important information by listening to numbers. As you watch the video again, fill in the numbers you hear in the spaces below.

1. Kobe is _____ miles east of Tokyo.

2. Kobe is a city of _____ million people.

3. _____ Americans live in Japan.

4. The flight landed in New York at _____ .

5. What are the phone numbers for the places listed below?

    a. Japanese Consulate _____

    b. U.S. Department of Defense _____

6. Where does the reporter tell people to call:

    a. if they have Japanese friends or relatives in Japan? _____
    _____

    b. if they have American friends or relatives in Japan?_____
    _____

    c. if they have American friends in the military in Japan? _____
    _____

Role Play

Do the following role-play activity in groups.

1. Work in groups of four or five.

2. One student in each group will be the reporter. The others in the group will be people who have survived.

3. Each group will choose one of the natural disasters from the reading. Discuss in your group what you would experience in such a disaster.

4. Plan a news report. The reporter will interview the survivors about their experiences in the disaster.

5. Practice your report a few times. Then, perform it for the class.

Writing About Natural Disasters

Write answers to the following questions. If you have never experienced a natural disaster, write answers about another emergency situation or use your imagination. In activity seven you will use your answers to write a story.

1. What kind of natural disaster were you in?

2. When did the disaster happen? How old were you?

3. Where were you living?

4. What were you doing when the disaster happened or when you heard the disaster was coming?

5. Who was with you?

6. What did you want to do?

7. What did you (or someone else) try to do?

8. How long did the emergency last?

9. How much damage was done?

10. What did you do after the disaster ended?

Natural disasters and emergencies can be scary and dangerous—just the kind of experiences that make a good story! Write a narrative about your experience using the answers to the questions above. Read your story to the class. Who had the most exciting experience?

Reading About Fire Emergencies

activity one

Preparing to Read

What do you know about fire emergencies? Your teacher will give you a few minutes to write down three things you know about the subject. Then, share your knowledge with the class.

activity two

Reading

Read the following information about fires.

Fire Facts

Sad but true:
- Most home fires occur when people are sleeping.
- A fire can destroy your home in five minutes.
- You have only minutes to escape.
- Over 6,000 people die in fires each year in the U.S.
- More than 28,000 are injured in fires each year in the U.S.
- 4.2 billion dollars are lost in home fires each year.
- 95% of home fires are accidents, as opposed to arson.
- The most common cause of house fires is smoking (cigarettes, lighters, etc.).

Here are some guidelines to prevent fires:
- Check your home for fire hazards. If you find any, remove them.
- Talk about fire safety with your family. Make sure that children know their addresses and telephone numbers. Everyone should also know the local emergency numbers to call.
- Make sure that children know how dangerous it is to play with matches or lighters.
- Have fire drills to practice getting out of the house.

If you are in a fire:
- Keep a cool head; panic is your worst enemy.
- Get everyone out of the house quickly. Stay close to the floor, because smoke and heat rise towards the ceiling. The best air is near the floor.
- Remember to STOP, DROP, and ROLL if your clothes catch on fire.
- Have an exit plan and use it.
- Call the fire department after you get out of the house.
- DO NOT GO BACK INTO THE HOUSE—NO MATTER WHAT!

Preventing Fires

There are three major fire hazards for house fires: electricity, heating units, and misuse of matches and lighters. Here are some rules to follow.

Electricity
- *Never* overload outlets. Don't plug in more than two cords into one outlet.
- Don't leave appliances plugged in when you're not using them.
- *Never* use appliances with cords that are damaged.

Heating Units
- *Never* leave space heaters on with no one in the room.
- Make sure that space heaters are *vented*; that is, that *there's room for the air to escape around them.*
- *Never* leave things that might catch on fire near heating vents or space heaters.
- If you have a fireplace, make sure there are doors or a screen in front of it when you use it.

Misuse of Matches and Lighters
- *Never* leave matches where children can get them.
- *Never* leave burning candles near things that will burn (such as curtains) or near children.
- *Never* smoke in bed.
- *Never* leave lit cigarettes in ashtrays.

Understanding the Reading

Thinking About the Reading

activity one

With your class or in small groups, discuss the following questions.

1. Look at the facts in the **Sad but true** box on page 87. Which fact was most surprising to you?

2. Look at the list in the **guidelines to prevent fires** box. Which things have you done? Which things do you need to do?

3. Read the list of fire hazards in the box on page 88. Which fire hazards existed in your home in the past? How did you remove them?

4. What do you think *STOP, DROP,* and *ROLL* means? Can you demonstrate these actions for the class?

5. If your home burned down and no one was hurt, what things would you miss the most? What would be the hardest (or impossible) to replace? Make a list, then compare your list to the lists of other groups.

6. What could you do to protect the things you listed in Question 5? Can you store important papers in a safe place? What about photographs?

Using a Map to Describe an Escape Plan

activity two

Every house or apartment should have an exit plan in case of fire. Everyone who lives there should know what the exit plan is and practice using it.

The sample plan below shows two ways for each person in the family to escape. The black arrows show the fastest way to get out of the house from each room. The white arrows show another way out if the windows in the bedrooms are blocked by fire.

EXAMPLE ESCAPE PLAN

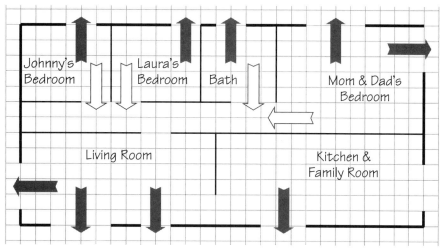

In the grid below, draw your house, apartment, or dorm room. Then add arrows to show how you (and others who live there) would escape in case of a fire. Remember to have two ways to get out in case the windows or doors are blocked. When you finish, describe your escape plan to your classmates.

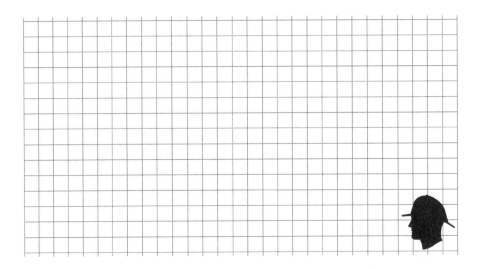

Learning about Emergency Equipment

Here are some items you might need in an emergency. Pictures of the items are on the next page. On the lines below, write down where you can buy them in your community. Put a check (✔) in front of the items you already have. Then, discuss the items with your classmates and teacher. Who has the greatest number of these items?

Do you have . . .   **Where can you buy this/them?**

☐ candles?   _____
☐ a flashlight?   _____
☐ a radio?   _____
☐ canned heat?   _____
☐ a camp stove?   _____
☐ extra batteries?   _____
☐ a smoke detector?   _____
☐ heavy tape?   _____
☐ canned (food) provisions?   _____
☐ bottled water?   _____
☐ a fire extinguisher?   _____

Preparing for Emergency Situations

Calling Emergency Numbers

In many communities in the U.S., there is one telephone number for many kinds of emergencies. You can call that number if you need the police, the fire department, or an ambulance. Usually the number is 911. When you call that number, the operator sends your call to the emergency service you need. Many communities have both 911 and individual numbers. Look in your local telephone book for these emergency numbers. Write them down so you will be ready in case of an emergency.

activity one

Work with a partner. **Student A** should read the **Situations** card on this page. **Student B** reads the **Situations** card on the next page. On each card, there are *two* situations: **reporting an emergency** and **receiving an emergency call.**

1. Take turns. Student A starts by reporting an emergency. Student B receives A's call, asks questions about the emergency, and writes down the information.

2. Then Student B reports an emergency, and Student A receives the call.

You might start your conversation like this:

B: Fire Department
A: Hello! I want to report a fire!

Student A: Situations

1. Reporting an emergency. There is a fire in your kitchen at home. Call the fire department. Tell the person at the fire department what the emergency is. Answer the person's questions.

- -

2. Receiving an emergency call. You are in charge of sending out ambulances. When someone calls, ask the following questions and write the information below. Then tell the caller that you will send an ambulance right away.

- What's your name?
- What's your address?
- What's the victim's (sick person's) name?
- What's the problem? Is the victim breathing? Is he conscious?
- What's your telephone number?

Name of caller: _____

Name of victim: _____

Address: _____

_____

Problem or symptoms: _____

Telephone number: _____

1. **Receiving an emergency call.** You work at a fire station. When someone calls, ask the following questions and write the information below. Then tell the caller that you will send a fire truck right away.
   - What's your name?
   - What's your address?
   - What's main street is near your address?
   - Where is the location of the fire? What part of your home?
   - What's your telephone number?

Name of caller: _____

Address: _____

_____

Main street near address: _____

Location of fire: _____

Telephone number: _____

- -

2. **Reporting an emergency.** Your best friend is lying on the floor, unconscious. He is breathing but you can't wake him up. Call an ambulance. Tell the person what the emergency is. Answer the person's questions.

Writing About Emergency Situations

R W L S
activity two

Work with a partner to do the following activity.

1. Choose an emergency situation from the list below. Get some information specific to your area. Think about the following questions:

Earthquakes

- How often do earthquakes happen in your area?
- When did the last bad one happen?
- Is there an earthquake plan at your school?

Tornadoes or hurricanes

- Are there any local warning systems? (For example, in some areas a loud siren sounds when a tornado is nearby.)
- Where is the safest place in your school?

Fires

- What is the escape plan for your school?
- Where are the fire extinguishers?

Car accidents

- What is the law in your area?
- When do you call the police?
- When do you ask for the other driver's license and insurance information?

Break-ins

- What do the police recommend to protect your house?
- What phone number do you call if your house has been broken into?

Winter Storms

- What is your school's closing policy in case of a storm?
- How will students know if the school is closed?
- Where can you get information about the roads?
- Who do you call if your electricity goes out?

2. Write a one-page information sheet for the other students in your school. Be sure to include the following:

- the name of the emergency or natural disaster

- a description of the emergency or natural disaster

- guidelines on what to do

- a list of emergency equipment people should have

- emergency phone numbers

- the names of radio or television stations that carry emergency information

If you have a computer available, input the information. Make the information look attractive and interesting. Perhaps you can include a drawing or make the information sheet into a brochure.

A Step Beyond

1. Make a safety check of your school. In groups, check the classrooms, office areas, lounges, restrooms, etc. Use the list of fire hazards as a checklist. Do you see any hazards in your school? Are things left plugged in? Discuss any hazards you find with your teacher and discuss ways to make your school safer. Then, write your ideas for improving school safety in several paragraphs.

2. Invite a local expert from the civil defense office or from a college or university to talk about regional natural disasters.

3. Arrange a visit to a senior citizen's center or apartment complex. Interview people who have lived in the community for a long time about the worst natural disaster they can remember. Or, interview a neighbor or friend.

CHAPTER seven

Health

in this chapter

You are going to read about and discuss different health issues, write a letter to a local health expert, and invite a guest speaker to your class to talk about health issues. The video segment is a TV news report about the flu in New York City. You will also complete a questionnaire and write an essay about stress in your life.

Getting Ready

activity one

Warming Up

Discuss the following questions with your class or in small groups.

1. What do you do to stay healthy?

2. What kinds of health problems have you had? What kinds of health problems have others in your family had?

3. How do you think the following things could affect your health:

   • being in the sun too much?

   • living with too much stress?

   • not getting enough sleep?

   • second-hand smoke (breathing in the smoke from other people's cigarettes)?

activity two

Brainstorming

As a class, brainstorm some health issues that people are concerned about today. As you suggest ideas, your teacher can write them on the board.

Reading and Presenting Information About Health Issues

Reading

You are going to read and present information about several health issues to your class.

1. Divide into four groups. Each group should be responsible for one of the following topics:

   a. Second-hand Smoke

   b. The Deadliest Skin Cancer

   c. How to Get a Good Night's Sleep

   d. Sexually Transmitted Diseases

2. You will find information about these four topics below. Everyone in your group should read the information about his or her topic thoroughly (this can be done at home or in class). Don't read about the other topics before the presentations.

3. In your group, make a list of all the important information in your passage. Ask your teacher about vocabulary that you don't know.

4. Decide how you can present the information to the rest of the class. (You might make a poster, for example.) Try to have everyone in your group participate in the presentation.

5. Prepare some discussion questions about your topic.

   Examples: How much time do you spend in the sun?
   How often do you breathe in second-hand smoke?

6. Make your group presentation to the class. During your presentation, the class members should take notes (see activity one: Taking Notes from Student Presentations on page 104). At the end of your presentation, ask your discussion questions.

Health Issues

Topic One: Second-hand Smoke

A   Are you a nonsmoker with friends or relatives who smoke? If you are, you may be breathing in "second-hand" smoke. This means that you inhale the smoke from other people's cigarettes. Scientists now think that living around second-hand smoke can cause as much lung damage as actually smoking ten cigarettes a day. The World Health Conference said that spending one hour in a room filled with smoke is the same as smoking one cigarette.

B　　Breathing in second-hand smoke causes your heart to beat faster and your blood pressure to go up. It also increases the level of carbon monoxide in your blood. Smoke from the lighted end of a cigarette (called "sidestream smoke") is especially dangerous because it contains much more carbon monoxide (CO), tar, nicotine, and ammonia than inhaled smoke does.

C　　The danger from second-hand smoke is greater for some people, especially the elderly and people with respiratory (breathing) or heart problems. Also, babies and children who live around smoke have more respiratory illness than children of non-smoking parents. Second-hand smoke increases a child's risk of getting pneumonia, bronchitis, or tonsillitis.

D　　Because of the dangers of second-hand smoke, at least thirty states in the U.S. have made laws limiting smoking in public places. In California, which has the strongest law, smoking is illegal in all restaurants and public buildings.

Topic Two: The Deadliest Skin Cancer

A　　Cancer can affect every part of your body, including your skin. In fact, the most common kind of cancer in the U.S. is skin cancer (450,000 new cases are diagnosed every year). Fortunately, it is the easiest of all cancers to find.

B

There are three main types of skin cancer. The two most common types, *basal-cell* or *squamous-cell,* can usually be treated easily. **Malignant melanoma** is much more dangerous. Every year, about 22,000 people in the U.S. develop melanoma and about 5,500 die from it. When melanoma is found early, it is easily cured. But if it is not found soon enough, it can be very difficult to treat. Unlike the other skin cancers, melanoma tends to spread to other parts of the body. If melanoma reaches the internal organs, it is much more difficult to treat. That is why melanoma can be deadly.

C

What causes melanoma? By far, the most important factor is too much exposure to the sun. The sun gives off ultraviolet radiation, which can cause severe damage to the skin. When you're exposed to the sunlight, the melanin in your skin increases to form a protective layer in the form of a suntan. Melanoma develops if the cells that produce melanin change into cancer cells that grow uncontrollably. Getting a tan can damage your skin. After the damage is done, it is permanent. The more your skin is damaged, the higher your chances of developing cancer.

D

Who is most likely to get melanoma? People who have fair skin are the most likely to develop melanoma, but people with all skin types can get it, too. Also people who live in sunny places are more likely to develop melanoma. For example, in the U.S., Arizona (in the desert area of the Southwest) has the highest rate of melanoma.

E

What can you do? To prevent melanoma, you should not spend too much time in the sun. When you are in the sun, use a sunscreen that is 15 SPF (sun protection factor) or higher.

F

Secondly, know your own skin. You should know what moles you have and watch for any changes in them. See your doctor at once if your moles change or if they have any of the following: mixed colors, irregular borders, asymmetry (one half does not match the other), or diameter greater than 6 millimeters.

Topic Three: How to Get a Good Night's Sleep?

A   The "average" adult gets between seven and eight hours of sleep each night, but different people need different amounts of sleep. If you usually wake up after only five or six hours and cannot go back to sleep, don't worry; this is probably as much sleep as you need. Many people think they need more sleep than they really do. There is usually no real problem if you wake up once or twice during the night. Research into sleep behavior shows that most people who think they get "hardly a wink" of sleep really get more rest then they realize.

B   Not getting much sleep for a few days will not hurt you if you can stay energetic and alert when you are awake. If you have insomnia (not being able to sleep) and it affects your daily activities, talk to a doctor. Insomnia is sometimes a sign of mental illness such as anxiety or depression. It can also affect how well you do your job. If you cannot relax into sleep when you go to bed, try some of the following suggestions.

1. Do not take work to bed with you. If you like to read in bed, do some light reading.
2. Do some physical exercise during the day so that your body feels tired enough to want the rest at bedtime. If you do not get enough exercise, try taking a walk a few hours before bedtime.
3. A warm bath just before bedtime may help you relax.

4. Make sure that your bed is comfortable and that you are not too hot or too cold. Most people sleep best in a room temperature of 60° to 65° F (16° to 18° C).
5. Use relaxation or meditation techniques.
6. If nothing works, get out of bed and stay up until you are tired. Then, go to bed and try to sleep. Be sure to get up at your regular time and try not to take a nap the next day.

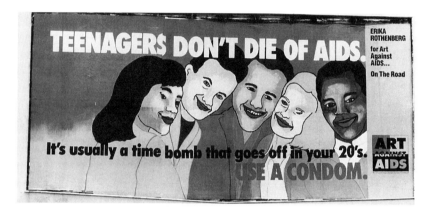

Topic Four: Sexually Transmitted Diseases

A   A sexually transmitted disease (STD) is an infection that goes from person to person during sexual contact. The way you are most likely to catch a STD is by having sexual intercourse with a partner who has it. Some STDs are bacterial infections (for example, gonorrhea, chlamydia, or syphilis). Others are viral (for example, herpes). AIDS (Acquired Immune Deficiency Syndrome), the most serious STD, results from a viral infection. Most STDs are curable, but AIDS has no cure and death is almost certain. Therefore, education about this disease is especially important.

B   Although AIDS can be spread when drug users share needles or, rarely, through blood transfusion, it is usually transmitted through sexual contact. AIDS is not considered to be very contagious; it is passed from one person to another through very close contact with infected blood or semen.

C   On the other hand, STDs such as gonorrhea, herpes and syphilis are very contagious, and many of them can be spread through brief sexual contact. However, none of these infections is spread during casual contact such as handshaking, talking, sitting on toilet seats, or living in the same house with an infected person. The microorganisms that cause STDs, including AIDS, all die quickly once they are outside the human body.

D   **How can you prevent STDs?** There is no vaccine for any of the STDs. The only sure way of preventing STDs and AIDS is by not having sex or by having a relationship with only one uninfected person (straight or gay). If you have several sexual partners, either heterosexual or homosexual, you are at high risk of getting some kind of STD. Also, correct use of a condom can lower the risk of getting AIDS and other STDs.

Understanding the Reading

Taking Notes from Student Presentations

activity one

As others in your group make their presentations, take notes on the important information about each topic.

Topic One: _____

_____

_____

_____

_____

_____

_____

_____

Topic Two: _____

_____

_____

_____

_____

_____

_____

_____

_____

Topic Three: _____

_____

_____

_____

_____

_____

_____

_____

_____

Topic Four: _____

_____

_____

_____

_____

_____

_____

_____

activity two

Writing Summaries

Using the notes you took, write short summaries (five to six sentences) for *two* of the health issues discussed in this activity. In a summary, you should write only the most important information, not all the details.

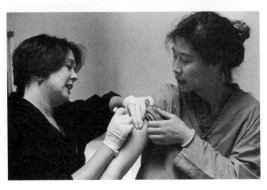

Watching a Video "The 'Flu' and Flu Shots"

Preparing to Watch

activity one

A common health problem people have every year is influenza, or "the flu." You are going to watch a TV news health report about the flu in New York City. Before you begin, discuss the following questions with your class.

1. Have you ever had the flu? What was it like? How long were you sick?

2. Do you ever get a flu shot? Do you think it's a good idea to get one?

3. What kind of medicine do you take for a cold or the flu?

4. What else do you do to get well?

Exploring Words

activity two

Before viewing the video, discuss the terms below with your teacher and the class. As you watch, notice how these words and phrases are used.

aches and pains

symptoms

the flu

respiratory ailment

chronic disease

First Viewing: Making Predictions

activity three

For the first viewing, watch the video segment without sound. As you watch the silent video, think about the questions below and fill in the following chart with your ideas. Compare your predictions with a partner. Then discuss your answers with your class.

1. What "scenes" or places are shown?

2. What people do you see?

3. What do you think the report will talk about?

4. What words or phrases might be used?

Scenes or places:	People:
What the report will talk about:	Words or phrases that might be used:

Second Viewing: Checking Your Predictions

activity four

Now watch the video with sound. Which predictions were correct? Which were not? Discuss the results with your class.

Writing About Health

Writing to a Health Expert

Write a letter to a local health expert—for example, to someone in your local health department. In your letter:

- tell the expert what kinds of things you have learned about in this unit

- ask for information about viruses, infectious diseases, and other health issues in your community

Use the form below to help you write. The sentences in the letter are suggestions only: You can create your own. Be sure to mail your letter!

Your address → _____
_____

Today's date → _____

Health expert's name → _____

Health expert's address → _____
_____

Dear _____ :
    My name is _____ and I am a student at
_____. My class is studying about different
health issues. We have learned about _____
_____
_____
_____ .
    I am writing to you because we would like to know more
about _____
_____ .
For example, one question I have is _____
_____ .
Another is _____
_____ .
    If you could write to us or send us some information,
we would appreciate it. Thank you very much.

Yours truly,

Sign your name → _____

Print your name → _____

Writing a Letter of Invitation

activity two

Invite a guest speaker from your campus health center or local health department to speak to your class. With your whole class, write a letter of invitation asking the person to talk about the health problems that are the most common in your area. Use your letter from the previous activity to help you. Tell the speaker other issues you would like to discuss.

Preparing for a Class Speaker

activity three

In groups, prepare questions to ask the speaker. Choose a specific student to ask each one. Use the topics and readings in this chapter to give you ideas for questions.

Writing a Thank-You Letter

activity four

When the speaker visits and lectures, listen attentively, take notes, and ask questions—the ones you prepared and any new ones that you can think of. After the visit, write a thank-you letter to the guest speaker. In your letter, tell what you learned from his/her visit.

Completing a Stress Questionnaire

Talking About Stress

activity one

Are you under stress? Medical research shows that as we live with more and more stress, we may have more health problems. Because stress can make our immune systems weaker, we may have more illnesses like colds and influenza. Discuss the following questions with your classmates and your teacher.

1. What is stress?

2. What causes stress?

3. What can be the result of living with too much stress?

4. When do you feel you are under a lot of stress?

Completing a Questionnaire

1. Complete the following questionnaire.

Questionnaire

How stressful is your life? Give yourself one to five points for each item:

     1 = almost always
     2 = often
     3 = sometimes
     4 = seldom
     5 = never

_____ **1.** I eat at least one meal a day that has all the basic foods needed for good health.

_____ **2.** I get seven to eight hours of sleep at least four nights a week.

_____ **3.** I give and receive affection regularly.

_____ **4.** I have at least one relative within fifty miles who can help me if I need help.

_____ **5.** I exercise at least twice a week.

_____ **6.** I smoke less than half a pack of cigarettes a day.

_____ **7.** I have fewer than five alcoholic drinks a week.

_____ **8.** I am the appropriate weight for my height.

_____ **9.** My income is enough to meet my basic expenses.

_____ **10.** I get strength from my religious beliefs.

_____ **11.** I regularly attend club or social activities.

_____ **12.** I have a group of friends and acquaintances.

_____ **13.** I have one or more friends to talk to about personal matters.

_____**14.** I am in good health (including eyesight, hearing, teeth).

_____**15.** I am able to speak openly about my feelings when angry or worried.

_____**16.** I have regular conversations with the people I live with about domestic problems—for example, chores, money, and daily living issues.

_____**17.** I do something for fun at least once a week.

_____**18.** I organize my time effectively.

_____**19.** I drink fewer than three cups of coffee (or tea or cola drinks) a day.

_____**20.** I take quiet time for myself during the day.

To find your score, add up the numbers you wrote down and subtract 20:

Total: _____ − 20 = _____

	If your score is . . .	you are . . .
Safe Zone	1. below 30	living a calm, unstressful life.
Leaving the Safe Zone	2. between 30 and 49	living with more stress than experts consider healthy. Maybe you should think about making some changes.
Moving near the Danger Zone	3. between 50 and 75	approaching the danger zone. Which of the twenty areas can you change?
Danger Zone	4. over 75	living with entirely too much stress. You may have serious problems as a result.

2. Work in pairs or small groups. Discuss your questionnaires. What areas can you change to make your life less stressful?

Writing About Stress

Preparing to Write

activity one

Think about the results of your stress questionnaire. Using the chart below, make some notes about each category. You will use your notes from the chart to create your first draft.

What Causes Stress in My Life	What I Do to Reduce Stress	What I Would Like to Change and How

Writing a First Draft

Use your notes from the chart to write an essay about the stress in your life. In your essay, try to tell about the following:

- the things in your life that cause you stress

- the things that you do to reduce stress

- what things you would like to change in order to reduce stress and how you might change them

Giving Feedback

After you have written the first draft of your essay, exchange papers with another student. Read the student's essay and answer the questions below about it. This feedback will help him or her write a better second draft.

1. Does the author talk about each category on the chart?

2. Where does the author need more explanation?

3. Does the essay need more examples? Where?

4. Draw a circle around the part of the essay you think is best. Write a note in the margin to explain why.

5. Do you have any suggestions for the beginning?

6. Do you have any suggestions for the conclusion?

7. Should the author change, move, or take out anything?

Writing a Second Draft

Meet with the person whose paper you read (and who read your paper). Explain your answers to the questions above to each other. Then rewrite your paper. As you rewrite, try to improve your paper based on your partner's feedback. Rewriting includes the following: adding, changing, moving, or deleting (taking out).

Writing a Final Draft

Read your new draft for errors in grammar, punctuation, or spelling. You should also get feedback from your teacher or another student. Finally, write your final draft. Make it as correct as possible.

> ***Alternative Writing Assignment:*** Discuss the results of your stress questionnaire with a partner. Then write a letter to your partner. Give advice about how s/he could have a less stressful life. Your partner will write a similar letter to you.

A Step Beyond

Arrange a trip to a health food store. Make a list of the kinds of products that you find there. Interview someone who works there. How do they choose the food items to sell? Why are some items there healthier than those in the grocery store?

CHAPTER eight

Entertainment and the Media

in this chapter

You will talk and read about different kinds of media. The video segment looks at some new developments in interactive TV services. After reading a television schedule, you will categorize different TV programs and keep a diary of the television programs that you watch. With your classmates, you will compare the results of your television diaries, then write a description of your favorite television show.

Getting Ready

Warming Up

The vocabulary words below are often used to talk about the different kinds of media. Some of the words are used for more than one form of media. A few words are slang; that is, informal. Draw lines to match the types of media on the left with the words on the right. There may be more than one match for each type of media. One is done for you.

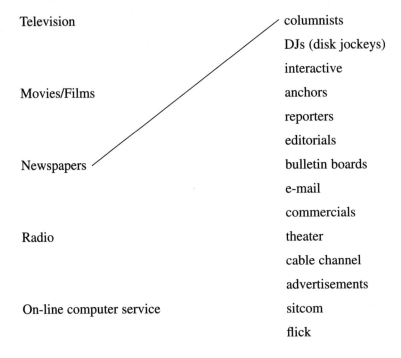

Television — columnists

DJs (disk jockeys)

interactive

Movies/Films — anchors

reporters

editorials

bulletin boards

Newspapers — e-mail

commercials

theater

Radio — cable channel

advertisements

On-line computer service — sitcom

flick

Work with another student and compare your answers. Do you have the same matches? Discuss your answers with the class and the teacher.

Reading About the Media

Preparing to Read

activity one

Discuss the following questions with your class or in small groups.

1. Do you learn about the news mostly by watching television or by reading the newspaper? What's different about news stories on television and in the newspaper?

2. Do you think people are more interested in international, national, or local news?

3. Do you think television is helping people learn about and understand other parts of the world?

Reading

activity two

Read the following article about interactive TV. As you read, think about the following questions.

1. Would you like to see any movie you want on TV, any time you want it?

2. According to the article, what are the problems with interactive TV?

3. Which services discussed in the article are you most interested in?

Video on Demand

A   Would you like to watch any movie you want, any time you want? Or play a computer game with a friend who lives several miles away? Or go shopping in a "video mall" where you can browse through the merchandise and order what you want? That's the promise of video-on-demand services that are now being tested in some areas. Video-on-demand means that communication over the TV is two-way: You send orders to the service and the service sends movies, TV shows, games, and other types of information and entertainment into your living room.

B   Many people can already order certain pay-per-preview movies offered by their cable TV companies. But they usually only have a choice of 7 to 10 movies a day and must watch them at the specific times they are shown. Video-on-demand puts you, the consumer, in control of the choices and schedule.

C   However, there are drawbacks to video-on-demand as it is now. You can pause a movie in the middle, unlike pay-per-view services, but you have to phone the company, punch in a code, and wait up to a minute for the movie to pause. This won't help you when you get an important phone call and don't want to miss any of the movie. Also, the services currently being tested offer only a limited number of shows. And, other features, such as shopping and video games, are now unavailable. Couch potatoes may have to wait a long time before video-on-demand is ready for prime time.

Understanding the Reading

Thinking About the Reading

activity one

Write answers to these questions. When you finish, discuss them with your class.

1. List three possible services of interactive TV.

_____

_____

_____

_____

2. What is the problem with ordering movies from video-on-demand services now?

_____

_____

Guessing Meaning from Context

activity two

Read the following sentences. Try to guess the meaning of the underlined words and phrases. Discuss them with your teacher if you need to. What words in each sentence help you to guess the meaning?

1. You should weigh both the <u>drawbacks</u> and the advantages before you make a decision.

2. John just sits on the couch all day watching TV. His wife calls him a "<u>couch potato</u>."

3. Just press the buttons on the remote control to <u>punch in</u> the channel you want.

4. There are many good TV shows on during the day, but most people watch TV from 8:00 to 11:00 P.M.—that's <u>prime time</u>.

activity three

Read the article again. Find and underline the words and phrases from activity two.

Using a Prefix to Make Opposites

activity four

We can change some words to their opposite meaning by adding the prefix *un-*. For example, in the last paragraph of the article, *unavailable* is the opposite of *available*. It means *not available*. Write the opposite of the words below by putting *un-* in front of the word. The first one is done for you.

1. important   not important =   _unimportant_____

2. happy   not happy =   _____

3. dependable not dependable = _____

4. believable   not believable =   _____

5. conscious   not conscious =   _____

6. afraid   not afraid =   _____

7. fortunate   not fortunate =   _____

Writing About Interactive TV

activity five

Which interactive TV service from question 1 in activity one on page 118 would you most like to have? Write a short paragraph about the service you want. Start by finishing the following sentence:

The interactive TV service I would most like to have is _____ because _____.

Add some more ideas about the service. When you are finished, read your answer to the class. How many people are interested in each service?

Watching a Video "Interactive TV"

Preparing to Watch

activity one

How has TV changed? You may remember what old TV sets looked like, or you may have seen pictures of them. Which of the phrases below describe TV in its early years in the 1950s and 1960s? Check (✔) the boxes. Discuss these phrases with your class and teacher.

☐ black and white picture

☐ rooftop antenna

☐ small screen

☐ 40 to 50 channels

☐ 24-hour programming

☐ snowy picture

☐ satellite dish

☐ cable connection

☐ remote control

Exploring Words

activity two

Before viewing the video, discuss the terms below with your teacher and the class. As you watch, notice how these words are used.

passive   to foresee

active   risk

Buck Rogers   to graze

activity three

Shopping by Television

In the United States and some other countries, many people receive a cable shopping service. On this channel, they can look at items, listen to a description, and order the items over the telephone. Have you ever bought something this way? Would you like to buy things this way? Why or why not? Discuss these questions with your class and teacher.

activity four

Listening for General Information

As you watch the video, try to answer the following questions. Circle the best answer.

1. How do the people in the video use their interactive TV service?
   a. by typing in commands on a computer
   b. by making choices from a list on the TV screen
   c. by telephone

2. Interactive TV services will come from
   a. private companies that make a profit from the services
   b. the government
   c. the TV networks such as CBS, NBC, and ABC

3. Interactive TV is for
   a. adults only
   b. children only
   c. the whole family

Describing an Interactive TV Service

activity five

Here's the main menu from the Main Street Interactive TV service:

Market Place
Money Manager
Family Game Time
Education
Travel
Gazette
Kidstuff

Imagine that you work for Main Street, and you are explaining the service to a possible customer. Choose one of the items from the menu above, and write a description of what the customer can do in that part of the interactive service. Use your imagination! When you finish writing, tell the class about your service.

Reading a Television Schedule

Discussing Television

activity one

You are going to look at a television schedule for Monday evening from 7:00 P.M. to 7:30 P.M. (Central Time). Or you can look at a local TV schedule from a newspaper or *TV Guide* magazine. As a class or in small groups, discuss the following questions with your classmates. This information will help you as you read the schedule on the next page.

1. What are television channels?

2. What is a television network?

3. Cable channels are shown in the TV schedule with abbreviations such as LIF for Lifetime, or by initials such as CNN (Cable News Network), MAX (Cinemax), HBO (Home Box Office). Can you think of any other cable channels? Which ones have you watched?

4. What is the difference between a *comedy* program and a *drama* program on television?

For details of premium-channel movies, see the guide following listings.

7PM
8PM

Monday

7PM (3)(4)(15) **THE NANNY (CC)** 9442
After Maxwell informs Fran (Fran Drescher) that his will names her as the kid's guardian, she loses her reasonably sound mind and believes he has a fatal heart condition. Doug Emerson: Michael Winters. (Repeat)

(5)(9) **FRESH PRINCE (CC)** ***1:00*** 61152
Hotshot Will thinks he's hot stuff as the manager of Ashley's budding singing career, but the rising star herself (Tatyana M. Ali) lets stardom go to her head after getting an enthusiastic response from record producer Gordy Berry (Obba Babatunde). Cameos by Quincy Jones and Little Richard. (Repeat)

(6)(7)(8)(13)(27) **MARSHAL (CC)—Crime Drama** ***1:00*** 41336
MacBride's assigned to protect a judge (Elizabeth Norment) who's received death threats, and discovers that she's been bribed—presumably by the same gang that's been threatening her. (Repeat)

Additional Cast

Villa Lobos..............................Miguel Sandoval
Stanley....................................Michael Massee
Niekrong...................................Erich Anderson
Cal...................................Callum Keith Rennie

(10) **EYEWITNESS (CC) Wildlife** 1220
A broad survey of horses ranges from why zebras have stripes (one is to ward off insects) to Athena's bridling of the winged Pegasus. [Ch. 10 is advising viewer discretion.]

(11)(19) **NATURAL WORLD (CC)** 5046/19626
"Gremlins of the Night" explores the nocturnal world of prosimians, a family of primates that includes such tree-dwellers as the tarsier, loris, bush baby and lemur. (Repeat)

(16)(30) **STAR TREK: VOYAGER (CC) Science Fiction** ***1:00*** 34046
When Voyager responds to a distress call from a Kazon vessel, they discover Federation technology on board, prompting Janeway (Kate Mulgrew) to suspect a traitor on her ship. Seska: Martha Hacket. (Repeat)

(24) **A DAY WITH (CC)** ***1:00*** 70404
A day in the lives of four celebrities follows model Elle Macpherson in London as she prepares to attend the British Academy Awards; the NBA's Dennis Rodman, who relaxes at a lake near Dallas; Matthew Perry ("Friends") in L.A. as he procrastinates with his writing partner on a script; and Ron Howard in a meeting with partner Brian Grazer.

(E) **NIGHTLY BUSINESS REPORT** 8370591
Commentator: Charles Schultze.

(A&E) **BIOGRAPHY** ***1:00*** 669133
Pocahontas (1595?-1617), the Virginia Native American princess who sought peace with the British settlers, and eventually married one.

(BET) **ROC (CC)—Comedy** 672133

(CNN) **NEWS (CC) Battista/Soles**

(DIS) **AVONLEA (CC)—Drama** ***:50*** 2843978
A visit from sharp-tongued Aunt Eliza (Kay Tremblay) disrupts the King household.

(DSC) **NATURAL WORLD** ***1:00*** 674065
A study of how humans have imperiled the African elephant's natural habitat.

(ESN) **STANLEY CUP CHAMPIONSHIP** ***3:00*** 127249
Game 5 (if necessary): New Jersey Devils at Detroit Red Wings. (Live)

(FAM) **EVENING SHADE (CC)—Comedy** 759220

(HBO) **MOVIE (CC)—Drama** ***1:35*** ★★ 8114713
"Boiling Point." Wesley Snipes.

(LIF) **UNSOLVED MYSTERIES** ***1:00*** 750084

(MAX) **MOVIE (CC)—Comedy** ***1:30*** ★ 527084
"The Beverly Hillbillies." Jim Varney.

(MTV) **PRIME TIME** ***2:00*** 432201

(NIK) **MISTER ED—Comedy** BW 608997

(SHO) **MOVIE (CC)—Drama** ***1:50*** ★ 6058336
"Double Impact." Jean-Claude Van Damme.

(TNN) **AT THE RYMAN—Music** ***1:00*** 506626
Graham Nash ("Unequal Love"), Kathy Mattea ("Ready for the Storm") and host Ricky Skaggs ("Cat's in the Cradle").

(TNT) **MOVIE (CC)—Thriller** ***3:00*** ★★★ 236412
"Jaws." (1975) Steven Spielberg's box-office blockbuster about an East Coast summer resort terrorized by a giant killer shark. Roy Schneider.

(USA) **MURDER, SHE WROTE (CC)—Mystery** ***1:00*** 203591

(WGN) **BASEBALL** ***3:00*** 237626
Pittsburgh at Chicago. (Live)

(WOR) **THAT GIRL—Comedy** 698171

7:05 (AMC) **MOVIE—Drama** ***2:10*** ★★ 536491
"Imitation of Life." Remake of the Fannie Hurst tear-jerker about the intertwined lives of two widowed mothers and their daughters. Lana Turner.

7:30 (3)(4)(15) **DAVE'S WORLD (CC)** 133927
Dave and Beth's risky land investment goes to pot when they discover that marijuana is growing on the site. Guard #1: Keith Golic. Dave: Harry Anderson. Beth: DeLane Matthews. (Repeat)

TV GUIDE/**103**

Reading a Schedule

Work in small groups. Discuss the questions below about the schedule on page 123. Write your answers to question 2 on the lines. If you need more information to answer the questions, ask your teacher.

1. Which shows on the schedule have you seen?

2. Pick five shows on the schedule that you would like to see. Rank them in order from 1–5 (1 = the show you would *most* like to see).

    _____

    _____

    _____

    _____

    _____

3. Public television doesn't show commercials and has more educational and news shows than the commercial channels. Which channels on the schedule do you think are public television channels?

4. Which channels show nature programs?

5. Find four drama programs. What time do they start? On what channels?

6. Which shows do you think are comedies? Why?

7. CC means "closed captioned." This means that some television sets can show on the screen the words that the actors are saying. Look for some shows marked CC on the schedule. Do you think closed captioning is a good idea? Why?

8. How many live sports broadcasts are on the schedule?

9. What do you think the stars (★) mean after the names of the movies? Which movie has the most stars? Why?

Classifying

Work in groups of three or four. Look at the categories of TV programs below. Find two programs that go in each of the categories. Write them in the spaces below. Your group should agree on the choices.

Comedy	Drama	News	Sports

Keeping a Television Ratings Diary

activity one

Listing Information

You are going to keep a diary of your television watching over the next week.* Each day, fill in the following chart with information about the programs you watch.

	Name of Program	Type of Program (News, Comedy, Sports, Movie)	Channel/Day/Time	Number of People in Your House/Apt. Watching	Name of Sponsors (Products Advertised)
Monday					
Tuesday					
Wednesday					
Thursday					
Friday					
Saturday					
Sunday					

activity two

Discussing What You Saw

Talk with your classmates about the different programs each person watched during the week. Find out the *three* programs watched by the *greatest* number of people in the class. List them here.

1. _____

2. _____

3. _____

*Or, your instructor may ask you to complete the diary over one *evening* of TV viewing only.

Explaining Your Choices

Tell your classmates which program on your list was the best. Explain why. Also, which was the worst and why? Ask the other students their opinions about the best and worst programs they watched.

Discussing Advertisements

Discuss the TV advertisements you saw. Were they interesting? Did they give any helpful advice? Were there too many?

Comparing Your Diaries

Compare the television diaries of all your classmates. Calculate how many programs of each of the following types your classmates watched. Then, discuss the results with your classmates. Which type of program was most popular with your class? Why? Which type do you think is most popular with people in your community?

Program Type	Number of Programs Watched
News	_____
Situation Comedy	_____
Movie	_____
Drama	_____
Soap Opera	_____
Documentary	_____
Cartoon	_____
Sports	_____
Other: _____	_____
_____	_____

Describing Your Favorite TV Show

Writing About Your Favorite TV Show

activity one

First, answer the questions below in complete sentences. Then, put your ideas together in two or three paragraphs.

1. What is the name of your favorite television show?

2. What kind of show is it: drama, comedy, adventure, news, documentary (real events filmed as they happen), sports, or some other type?

3. Who are the people on the show?

4. What do they do on the show?

5. Where does the show take place?

6. What do you like best about the show?

7. What do you think could be better about the show?

Sharing Your Writing

activity two

Read the description to your group or to the class. Listen to the other descriptions. Which shows do you want to watch?

A Step Beyond

Sometimes museums can provide information about television and broadcasting. Three types of museums that do are science museums, moving image museums, and broadcasting museums. Take a field trip to your local museum and try to find new information on television.

Try to arrange a trip to your local PBS (Public Broadcasting Station) television station. Find out if they provide tours and, if possible, take a field trip there. Write about what you learn.

CHAPTER nine

Social Life

How important is your social life? Doctors tell us that people who have friends and an active social life live longer. In this chapter, you are going to explore some different aspects of social life, including dating, marriage, and friendships. In the video segment, several people talk about how to find a mate and about what to do—and what not to do—on a date. You will also write a short speech about friends and social life and give your speech to the class.

in this chapter

129

Getting Ready

Warming Up

This is a happy person with an active social life.

This pie chart shows how she divides her social life.

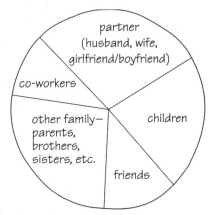

In Circle A, draw a pie chart showing your social life *now*. Make the biggest parts the ways you spend most of your time.

In Circle B, draw a pie chart showing your *ideal* social life. Make the biggest sections of the chart the most important parts of the social life you want.

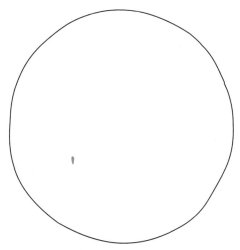

Circle A: Your Social Life Now

Circle B: Your Ideal Social Life

Discussing Your Social Life

activity two

Tell the class one of the ways that an ideal social life would be different from your social life now. Discuss it. Can you make your social life better? What can you substitute for the parts you don't have?

Reading About Dating

Exploring Words

activity one

A romantic partner (husband, wife, boyfriend, girlfriend) is an important part of many people's social lives. Dating services are businesses that help men and women meet people to date and, perhaps, marry. Dating services use questionnaires and sometimes computer analysis to do this.

The dating service you are going to read about is called Ebony, Inc. Three meanings for the word *ebony* are:

1. a very valuable wood that is very dark in color
2. the color black
3. the name of a magazine with articles and advertisements primarily aimed at African Americans

Discuss the words below with your teacher and the class. Some of them are informal or slang. As you read the article on the next page, notice how these words and phrases are used.

biographical	monogamous
to spot	branch
a bunch of people	a bad rap
downside	a brother
materialistic	Mr. Right

Scanning for Information

activity two

Before you read the article, try to find answers to the following questions as quickly as you can. Look for capital letters and numbers to help you find the information you need. Your teacher will tell you when to start looking and when to stop.

1. What is the name of the president of The Ebony Connection?
2. Where is The Ebony Connection located?

3. How much did Jill Hammond pay to join The Ebony Connection?

4. How many people belong to The Ebony Connection?

5. What does Darrin Wells do for a living?

6. How many women has Darrin Wells met through The Ebony Connection?

Helping Love Along: College Park Dating Service Lets Blacks Connect

ZeEster Clyatt

When Jill Hammond first spotted her possible husband-to-be, she was looking at a color photograph. She also read some information about him and a personal interview he had with a matchmaker. Those were the services the 32-year-old accountant received from The Ebony Connection. She paid $500 for a one-year membership. The Ebony Connection was started by Gabe Essic, the president and general manager. It is the only African-American dating service in Atlanta.

"If things continue the way that they are, we probably will be married in a year or so," Hammond said of the 33-year-old soldier she met through the dating service.

The Ebony Connection has about 300 members—48 percent male and 52 percent female. Members like Hammond, who believe they have met Mr. Right, are allowed to freeze their membership (remain members without paying) for up to two months. The Ebony Connection also offers counseling. The service is strictly heterosexual, but Essic warned that it's impossible to screen for sexual preference. He also said HIV testing of members is "unrealistic" because they could go out and have unprotected sex on the days after being tested. "We ask each and every member to be adults and to practice safe sex, if indeed it gets to that point," he said. Essic said 80 percent of the members are highly educated, and many are professionals or business executives. The youngest member is 24, and the oldest is 60.

Essic started the business a year and a half ago, and so far, he said, the response has been "tremendously great." Hammond said it's unfortunate that dating services have gotten a bad rap. "You see these ads on TV and you get this perception of a bunch of single people that want to get together and have wild sex. That's not what The Ebony Connection is about," she said.

Darrin Wells, 41, is government auditor and single father, raising his 13-year-old son alone. So far, he's met seven different women, one of whom is now his steady girlfriend. He said the downside to the dating service is that it tends to attract women who are materialistic. "They won't look at a brother who doesn't have certain things," Wells said. When Wells found The Ebony Connection, he recalled saying to Essic, "If you can find me somebody that I can date and have a monogamous relationship with, I'll pay you to do it."

Understanding the Reading

Thinking About the Reading

activity one

Circle the answers to these questions.

1. Jill Hammond is
    a. 24 years old
    b. 32 years old
    c. 33 years old
    d. 60 years old

2. The man she is probably going to marry is
    a. Gabe Essic
    b. John Right
    c. a 33-year-old soldier
    d. Darrin Wells

3. Members of The Ebony Connection
    a. include more men than women
    b. are 80% HIV-positive
    c. are mostly interested in wild sex
    d. range in age from 24 to 60

4. Members can freeze their membership for two months because
    a. they should know by then if they've met the right person or if they need to meet more people
    b. they might be meeting only materialistic people
    c. they have to take an HIV test
    d. they are only interested in dating people for two months

Matching

Match the five quotes with the person who said each one. Write the name of the person on the line.

> Gabe Essic, *owner of The Ebony Connection dating service*
>
> Jill Hammond, *accountant and customer of The Ebony Connection*
>
> Darrin Wells, *government auditor and customer of The Ebony Connection*

1. Response to the dating service has been "tremendously great."

_____

2. The Ebony Connection is not for "a bunch of single people who want to get together and have wild sex."

_____

3. ". . . we will probably be married in a year or so."

_____

4. Testing members for HIV is "unrealistic."

_____

5. Some women won't consider dating "a brother who doesn't have certain things."

_____

Talking About Dating Services

Discuss the following questions in groups of three or four. Have one person in your group take notes on the group's answers. Your teacher may ask you to report your answers to the class.

1. Why do you think people like Jill Hammond and Darrin Wells need to pay a company to find dates for them?

2. Do you think this is a good way to find people to date or to marry?

3. Which of the following factors do you think dating services should consider when matching people? Check (✔) the boxes.

☐ age ____

☐ educational background ____

☐ profession ____

☐ ethnic background ____

☐ religion ____

☐ height ____

☐ interests ____

☐ desire to have children ____

☐ personality ____

4. What factors in the list above are important to you in choosing a husband or wife? Rank them from 1 for most important to 9 for least important. Write the numbers on the lines above.

Watching a Video "Finding a Mate"

activity one

Exploring Words

Before viewing the video, discuss the terms below with your teacher and class. As you watch, notice how these words and phrases are used.

trial and error
matchmaker
classified ads
to compliment
to cling
to pick up the tab

First Viewing: Listening for General Information

In this video, several people talk about the following topics:

 a.   What to do before you look for a mate

 b.   Using a dating service

 c.   Placing a personal ad

 d.   Knowing what to do and what not to do on a date

As you watch the video, think about these things:

 1.   Notice that all the couples in the video are holding hands. Is this common for couples in your culture? What do you think of people holding hands and kissing in public?

 2.   Watch each of the following people who are interviewed:

   Dr. Jim Sulas, *professional matchmaker*

   Victoria Parker, *owner of a San Diego dating service*

   Judy Knowle, *professional writer of personal newspaper ads*

   Listen for the advice that they give.

Second Viewing: Listening for Specific Information

Draw lines to match the people on the left with the advice on the right:

"If you write negative things, you'll attract negative people."

Jim Sulus   "Women sometimes expect too much from their dates."

"Think positive thoughts, not negative ones."

Victoria Parker   "Looking confident is important."

"Creative ads work best."

Judy Knowle   "Do things you enjoy and you'll attract people."

"Men should dress well and attract well-dressed women."

In small groups, discuss which advice you agree with and which you don't. Report your ideas to the class.

Third Viewing: Classifying and Listing Information

activity four

Watch the video again and do the following activity.

1. What qualities in a mate mentioned in the video do you like? What qualities don't you like? While watching the video, list them in the chart below.

Like	Don't Like

2. Compare lists with a partner. Are your lists similar? Are they different?

3. Discuss your lists in groups of four. Do you agree with the speakers in the video? Do you like and not like the same things as the other members of your group?

4. Add at least two items to the list of things you think people like and don't like about their dates or spouses.

Defining Friendships

Discussing Friends

activity one

Decide what qualities a friend should have and what kinds of things a friend should do. Look at the list on the next page. Write "yes" beside the things that you expect from a friend or that you would do for a friend. Write "no" beside the things you do not expect from a friend or would not do for a friend. Leave a blank if you are not sure.

A friend would/should:

____ lend you a small amount of money.

____ lend you more than $50.

____ give you a ride when it's convenient.

____ give you a long distance ride (to the airport, across town, etc.).

____ take you shopping.

____ stay with you when you are sick.

____ bring you food, medicine, and other things you may need when you're sick.

____ help you with your homework.

____ help you during an exam.

____ take care of your children for a few hours.

____ take care of your children for a few days if you go away.

____ give you a present for your birthday or special holiday.

____ come visit in your home with you and your family.

____ be honest about your appearance.

____ disagree with you about politics, religion, etc.

____ be of the same sex as you.

____ help you with housecleaning.

____ shake your hand when you meet.

____ kiss you when you meet.

____ hug you when you meet.

____ talk with you about personal feelings.

____ talk with you about personal problems.

____ call before they come to visit.

Talking About Your Ideas

activity two

Compare your answers with those of other members of your class. Answer the following questions:

1. If there are people from different countries in your class, can you find some cultural differences in their answers? (For example, in some countries people kiss when they meet; in others, they don't.)

2. If there are people from the same country in your class, are there differences in their answers? Discuss why these answers are different.

Making a Short Speech

R *W*
activity one

Choosing a Topic

Make a short speech about friends and social life. Your speech should last for about two to three minutes. Choose one of the topics from the list that follows. Take a few minutes to organize your ideas on the topic for your speech. Make some notes.

Topics

1. What are the three most important qualities in a friend?

2. What are three ways to make friends?

3. Is marriage necessary anymore?

4. Is it important to know a person for a long time before getting married?

5. What kind of behavior between men and women is permissible before marriage?

6. What is the best friendship you have ever had?

7. What are worthwhile (good) ways to spend your free time?

8. What rules should teenagers have to obey?

9. Should you let your teenage sons and daughters go to nightclubs?

10. Would you let your sons and daughters study in the United States or Canada?

11. What kinds of activities do high school students in your country normally participate in and how often?

12. What are the three most important qualities in a wife/husband?

13. Is it valuable to have friends of a different race or religion and, if so, why?

14. What is the ideal social evening?

15. How do your friends irritate you?

16. What are three things that would destroy a friendship?

activity two

Organizing Notes/Making a Speech

Organize the notes that you took for activity one in an outline form so that you can easily express your ideas. Write a short introduction and conclusion. Speak to your class about the topic that you chose.

activity three

Listening to Speeches

Take notes from other students' speeches. Afterwards, summarize the three best speeches or write a one-sentence summary of each speech.

activity four

Writing Your Speech

Write your speech, using your outline and notes from activity two. Remember these differences between good speeches and good writing:

- Speeches are shorter and contain simpler sentences because people usually can't understand as much when listening as when reading.

- Speeches signal their organization more clearly to help listeners follow. For example, someone giving a speech might say "I want to discuss three points. First . . . Second . . . Finally."

- Speeches often contain more repetition of ideas and words to make a greater impact on the listener.

Giving Advice: Dear Student

activity one

Discussing Problems

Our friends, family, and social life often give us the greatest joy in living. But, they also sometimes present us with the hardest problems. Everyone needs some advice from time to time. Have you ever seen advice columns in a newspaper? Try to look at an advice column such as *Dear Abby* or *Ann*

Landers before doing this exercise. You are going to write answers to letters describing problems that people are having.

Read the following letters which describe problems. What do you think the person(s) in each situation should do? Write a letter in response to each problem.

Love Problems

Dear Student,

I'm in love with a woman from another country (she's also of a different religion). We would very much like to get married. I'm 26 and she's 24. The problem? My parents are absolutely against it. They think I will be doing something very stupid if I marry her. What should I do?

— In Love and Confused

Dear In Love,

_____

_____

_____

_____

_____

_____

Roommate Problems

Dear Student,

My roommate is very nice, but we're having some problems getting along. My roommate likes to play loud music, and it disturbs me when I'm studying. Also, I like to stay up late at night, but my roommate goes to sleep early and wants all the lights off. What should we do?

— Roomie

Dear Roomie,

_____

_____

_____

_____

_____

Drinking and Driving

Dear Student,

    My boyfriend and I have been going out for about six months. I like him, and we enjoy each other's company. The problem is that he really likes to drink. Sometimes he has five or six drinks and then gets into the car to drive me home. When he drinks and drives, I'm really afraid. I want to say something, but I don't know what to say. Should I offer to drive? (I'm a good driver.) Or should I insist on driving?

                          — Frightened on Saturday Nights

Dear Frightened:

_____

_____

_____

_____

_____

Marriage Problems

Dear Student,

    I've been married for five years and I'm very happy, but there's just one thing that bothers me. My husband never remembers to get me a card or present for my birthday or Valentine's Day. I always plan special dinners for his birthday, invite friends over, and get him a nice present, but he never does anything for my birthday. Every year, I wait for him to do something, but then I get sad and cry. He says he just doesn't care about birthdays, and I shouldn't get so upset, but I can't help it. I love him very much, and we get along really well the rest of the year. Is there any way to solve this problem?

                          — Sad and Forgotten

Dear Sad and Forgotten:

_____

_____

_____

_____

_____

Using a Chart to Compare Advice

Discuss the problems in groups of three or four. Compare your answers with the other students in your group. In the chart below, list the advice that each student gives. One possible answer is given as an example.

	Student One	Student Two	Student Three
Love Problems	Marry her if you love her.		
Roommate Problems			
Drinking and Driving			
Marriage Problems			

Discussing Your Advice

Share your advice with the class. Your teacher may list the advice on the chalkboard and read your letters to the class.

Reading

A newspaper in Atlanta, Georgia, published a series of articles about how people met and got married. Each article had the same parts as the one on the next page. Read the article. Pay attention to the information in each part.

NEWLYWEDS: *Reluctance Turns To Romance*

Martha Woodham

Renée Heard Thomas and Derrick Thomas. Renée, 35, is a special agent with the federal government; Derrick, 41, is a flight attendant with Delta Air Lines.

How they met: A mutual friend, Leonard Patterson, decided Renée and Derrick would be perfect for each other, ignoring their protests that they weren't interested in the dating scene. Both were happy with their single lives, but Leonard kept pestering them to get together.

Finally, Derrick gave in. About eighteen months ago, he called Renée, who agreed to meet him at a Waffle House restaurant on a Saturday morning. "I didn't want him to come to my house," Renée says. "I didn't want him to take me to dinner to try to impress me."

So they met, and Derrick accompanied her while she ran errands. "What kind of a date was that?" Derrick asked. He finally talked her into having lunch at the Black-Eyed Pea. Despite their misgivings, they became friends.

Let's get married: At midnight on Christmas Eve, 1993, Derrick invited Renée into the living room and sat her down in front of the fire. He serenaded her with "Lady," the Kenny "Baby-face" Edmonds song, then knelt to ask her to marry him.

"I looked into his eyes and started crying and crying and crying and crying," Renée says. "I thought she was going to say no because she couldn't stop crying," Derrick says.

Our wedding day: July 5 at Couples Only Resort in Jamaica

Our wedding style: The couple shared vows in a gazebo surrounded by flowers. "It was very colorful and romantic," Renée says.

Something old, etc. Renée borrowed a friend's long white gown.

Uniquely ours: The couple asked the minister to read Ephesians, Chapter 5, their favorite Bible passage about marriage.

Our favorite wedding tradition: Renée and Derrick loved leaving their tropical wedding on a sailboat.

Our favorite gift: The couple treasure a fifteen-inch candle made by Renée's sister. The white candle, set on a base of white flowers, has their wedding photograph laminated on it.

Let's party: Although there was a small reception, complete with Jamaican wedding cake, the couple really celebrated their small marriage once they were back in Atlanta. On Sept. 24, they gave a party for 300 at the Fort McPherson Officers' Club.

Personal touches: Derrick's daughter, Brittanie, 15, greeted guests. His son, Sterling, 11, was also part of the festivities.

Honeymooning: The couple spent seven days in Jamaica.

After the wedding: The couple now lives in Austell.

Writing About a Wedding

Notice the headings in the newspaper article. They explain the kind of information in each part. Using the same headings, write a story of the wedding of someone you know. If you are married, you can write about your own wedding. Or, you can interview your parents or friends to get information about their wedding. Use these headings:

Names and occupations of the bride and groom:

How they met:

Let's get married (How they decided to get married):

Our wedding day (When and where the couple married):

Our wedding style (What kind of ceremony they had—formal, indoor, outdoor, etc.):

Something old, etc. (A tradition in American weddings is that the bride should wear "something old, something new, something borrowed, something blue." This section tells how the bride carried out this tradition):

Uniquely ours (How their wedding ceremony was different from others):

Our favorite wedding tradition (The part of the wedding ceremony they liked best):

Our favorite gift (The present they liked the most):

Let's party (A description of the reception party after the wedding ceremony):

Personal touches (Special things they did for the wedding ceremony):

Honeymooning (Where the couple went on their honeymoon—the trip after the wedding):

After the wedding (Where the couple lives now):

Share your stories with the class. Who had the most unusual wedding?

A Step Beyond

Interview three students in your class about their social lives. Ask them questions, such as:

1. What kind of movies do you like?

2. What are your hobbies?

3. Who are your closest friends?

4. What do you do to have fun?

5. What kind of books do you like to read?

Write a story about one person that you interviewed. Or write a speech about the person and present it to the class.

CHAPTER ten

Customs, Celebrations, and Holidays

in this chapter

People in all countries of the world celebrate special events and holidays. Some celebrations seem to be universal—marriages, for example. Other celebrations are related to religious, national, or cultural events. You are going to talk and read about different holidays and celebrations. In the video segment, you will watch scenes from a parade in Harlem in New York City. And you will write a description of your favorite holiday.

Getting Ready

activity one

Warming Up

Work in groups of three. In your group, choose one of these events:

birthday   graduation   parade

wedding   funeral   fair or festival

Write ten words about the event you choose. Then, read your list to the class. Do not say which event your group chose. Can the class guess the event?

activity two

Discussing Celebrations

Discuss the following questions with your group or the whole class.

1. What events does your family celebrate?

2. Which celebration do you like best?

3. What is your favorite part of these celebrations? Look at the list below.

   • the change from your daily routine

   • the chance to do something with your family

   • the special foods

   • the presents

   • the religious ceremony

   • something else: _____

Reading About Holidays and Celebrations

activity one

Preparing to Read

Discuss the following questions with your class or in small groups.

1. Why do you think people enjoy holidays and celebrations?

2. Have you ever celebrated a holiday with people from another culture? Did you enjoy it? Did you understand why that holiday was important to them?

Reading

activity two

Read the following article about holidays and celebrations.

Celebrations and the Multicultural Society

A   Why do all countries and cultures have holidays and celebrations? Anthropologists—people who study cultures—say that these celebrations are important because they help people to understand their own cultures.

B   Celebrations may have religious, political, or other special meanings for the people of a culture. The activities, food, and decorations of a particular holiday remind people of the history they share with other members of their culture. So sharing these celebrations is more than a fun time for the members of a culture: It helps to connect them as a group.

C   This group connection is important, but it can have both good and bad results. Sometimes people have to join together to protect their culture from outside attack—for example, in a time of war. However, one culture can also fight with another culture because of differences in religion, language, or customs. When members of one culture do not respect the differences of members of another culture, war and tragedy can result.

D   Today, many people believe that different cultures can live together in one country. They believe that members of different cultures can respect each other's differences without changing their own customs and beliefs. In the United States, this idea is called a multicultural society.

Chapter 10 • Customs, Celebrations, and Holidays

149

| E | However, other people think that having many different cultures within one country is dangerous. They think that people from different cultures will not defend the country in time of war because of their different beliefs, languages, and customs. These people believe that everyone in a country should share the language, customs, and values of the majority of the people—the culture that has more than 50% of the population. |
| F | What do you think? |

Understanding the Reading

Exploring Words

activity one

Read the words and phrases below. In each paragraph, find a word that has the same meaning. Write the word on the line after the paragraph letter.

Words and Phrases	Paragraph	
1. learn the meaning of something	A	_____
2. bring or join together	B	_____
3. save	C	_____
4. a terrible, sad event	C	_____
5. fight for	E	_____
6. beliefs about what is good and bad	E	_____

Using Context to Understand Vocabulary

activity two

Sometimes a writer will define a vocabulary word in the text to help the reader understand it. One way to do this is to put the definition after a dash (—). Read the following sentence.

I bought a new ottoman—a small stool for resting my feet.

In the sentence, the phrase "a small stool for resting my feet" is a definition for *ottoman*. Look for two definitions after dashes in the reading. Write the definitions on the lines below.

1. anthropologist _____

2. majority _____

activity three

Finding Main Ideas

In essays written in English, every paragraph should have a main idea. The writer does not always state the main idea directly. Match each of the main ideas below with the correct paragraph from the reading. Write the number of the main idea on the line beside the correct paragraph.

___ Paragraph A   1. Some people believe in a mulitcultural society.

___ Paragraph B   2. Feeling strongly about one's culture can be good or bad.

___ Paragraph C   3. Holidays and celebrations strengthen people's connections to their culture.

___ Paragraph D   4. Some people don't like the idea of a multicultural society.

___ Paragraph E   5. Holidays and celebrations help people to understand their culture.

Watching a Video "A Cultural Celebration"

activity one

Preparing to Watch

What do you think of when you hear the word *parade?* Make a list of words or phrases. Your teacher or another student should write them on the chalkboard. Here are a few examples:

parade = decorated floats, bands, celebrating, crowded

Exploring Words

Before viewing the video, discuss the terms below with your teacher and the class. As you watch the video, notice how these words are used.

route

African American

theme

popularity

die-hards

vendor

First Viewing: Listening for General Information

The video shows a parade in Harlem, a largely African-American community in New York City. This annual parade celebrates the culture and history of Harlem and of African Americans in the United States.

Read these questions before you watch the video. Think about them as you watch. Then discuss them with your class.

1. When speaking about the African-American Day Parade, the first speaker says "It's a black thing. If you're black, you understand it."

   What do you think he means?

2. A group of young people chant:

   "Who are we?" "Colonial Park!"

   "How are we living?" "Drug free!"

   Why do you think this group is a part of the parade?

3. The two men who are walking in the parade are David Dinkins, the former mayor of New York City, and Jesse Jackson, a well-known politician and religious leader in the U.S. (he ran for president in 1988).

   Why do you think they are participating in the parade?

Second Viewing: Listening for Specific Information

Listen to what two speakers and the narrator say. Fill in the blanks below.

1. The woman in the curlers:

   "What I like about the parade, it's part of our _____. It teaches the _____ _____ our culture."

2. The man with the cap:

"What I like and enjoy _____ is seeing the kids participating and _____ and a variety of our African-American brothers and _____ coming down and showing what our community is made of—positive stuff."

3. Narrator:

"Marchers relax from all that _____ by shopping at a vendors' market set up especially for this day _____ with African goods."

activity five

Describing a Parade

Describe a parade you have seen. What was the purpose of the parade? Were there vehicles (cars, trucks, floats, etc.) in the parade? Were they decorated? What did the people wear? Was there music? Read your description to the class, and then answer any questions your classmates have about it.

Learning About Holidays in the United States

activity one

Matching

Work in pairs or groups of three and do the following activity.

1. Look at the pictures on the next page. Read the descriptions of the holidays. Ask your instructor about any vocabulary you don't understand.

2. Match each description with one of the pictures. Write the number of the picture in the box next to the correct description. Your group must agree on the matches.

New Year's Day, *January 1*

1.

Purpose:	to celebrate the beginning of a new year
Customs:	People have parties at home or in restaurants on New Year's Eve. People stay up until midnight to greet the New Year. Some people have parties in their homes on New Year's Day; they eat "buffet" meals, where they help themselves to whatever dishes they like; a lot of people watch football games on TV.
Symbols:	an old man with a sickle (a harvest tool) represents the old year; a baby represents the New Year
Foods:	champagne and snacks on New Year's Eve; in the South, people eat black-eyed peas for good luck on New Year's Day
Open:	hospitals, airports
Closed:	banks, post offices, most stores and restaurants, offices, schools

Presidents' Day, *Third Monday in February*

2.

Purpose:	to celebrate the birthdays of George Washington and Abraham Lincoln
Customs:	no real celebration, but many people have the day off from work
Symbols:	cherries
Foods:	Some people eat cherry pie in honor of George Washington.
Open:	stores (often there are big sales on winter items), restaurants
Closed:	banks, post offices, some offices, schools

Memorial Day, Fourth Monday in May

3.

Purpose:	to remember soldiers who died in war
Customs:	parades; some people put flowers on graves of soldiers; some people display the United States flag outside their homes
Symbols:	none
Foods:	none
Open:	stores, restaurants
Closed:	banks, post offices, some offices, schools

☐ **Independence Day, July 4**

Purpose:	to celebrate the signing of the Declaration of Independence, which separated the United States from England in 1776
Customs:	fireworks after dark, picnics, barbecues, parades
Symbols:	United States flag, Uncle Sam (the U.S. symbol, a thin man in a suit with a beard and a tall hat with a band of stars), the colors red, white and blue
Foods:	watermelon, food cooked outside on a grill
Open:	stores, restaurants
Closed:	banks, post offices, some offices, schools

4.

☐ **Halloween,** *October 31*

Purpose:	to celebrate the night before All Saints' Day (people used to believe that evil spirits came out on this night)
Customs:	Children dress in costumes and go from house to house saying "Trick or Treat"; people give them candy. Adults sometimes dress in costumes and go to parties. People carve faces on pumpkins to make jack-o'-lanterns.
Symbols:	witches, ghosts, pumpkins, the colors orange and black
Foods:	pumpkin pie, candy corn
Open:	everything
Closed:	nothing

5.

☐ **Thanksgiving,** *Fourth Thursday in November*

Purpose:	to remember a feast held by the first English settlers (called "Pilgrims") in Massachusetts after their first year's harvest (1621); Native Americans brought corn, turkeys, and deer. The Pilgrims gave thanks for surviving a very difficult year in their new home.
Customs:	Families gather—sometimes from long distances—for a big meal. They usually give thanks for being together and other blessings.
Symbols:	pilgrims, sheaves of wheat (wheat plants), dried corn, pumpkins, turkeys
Foods:	turkey, stuffing, sweet potatoes, corn, mincemeat or pumpkin pie, squash
Open:	hospitals, airports
Closed:	almost everything

6.

Making a Poster Presentation

Work in groups. Choose one holiday on pages 154 and 155, another American holiday, or a holiday from your country or culture.

1. Find out more information about your holiday. For example, look in an encyclopedia or magazine in the library. If possible, ask some people how they celebrate the holiday. You may find that people celebrate the holiday in different ways.

2. Prepare a poster about your holiday. First, paste or draw pictures of your holiday on a large piece of paper or poster board. Then, add some written information. Be sure to include the following:

   • when the holiday happens

   • the history or beginning of the holiday

   • how people celebrate the holiday

   Include information about how families celebrate this holiday (or a holiday similar to it) in your culture. You can use more than one poster board if you want.

3. Choose one person to be the "presenter." This person will stand by the poster. When all the posters are displayed around the room, the presenter will tell people about the holiday.

4. People who are not presenters will be "information gatherers." They should move around the room, looking at all the posters and listening to the presenters. Information gatherers should complete the chart below with information about what they read and hear.

Holiday	Purpose	Customs	Foods	Symbols	Other

Discussing Holidays

Discuss the following questions with the class.

1. Do you celebrate any of the holidays in activity two with your family?

2. In the United States, most workers get nine to ten paid holidays a year when they don't have to work, plus two or three weeks of vacation. Is this enough time off? Do you know of workplaces where workers get more days off for holidays and vacation? Fewer days?

Classifying Information

Make a list of all the holidays celebrated by your classmates. Add any holidays you know about from other countries and cultures. Then, working with a partner, try to put the holidays in the best category below. Some holidays may fit more than one category.

Religious	Political	Cultural	Historical

Writing About Holidays

Thinking About a Main Idea

You are going to write a description of your favorite holiday for the other members of your class. Think about what you need to tell your classmates so they understand why this is your favorite holiday.

First, you need to think about your main idea. Try finishing the following sentence:

_____ is my favorite holiday because _____

_____

_____

_____

Make a general statement about the meaning or customs of the holiday, but don't include specific information about what you do or eat on that day. Your instructor will ask you to read your sentence and may write it on the board. Listen to the sentences the other students wrote. Which one makes you want to know more? Which one makes you want to read the rest of the paper? Discuss this with your teacher and the class. Then, decide if you want to rewrite your sentence to make it more interesting.

Preparing to Write

Write the answers to the following questions in a sentence or two. You will use your answers to write an essay.

1. What is the name of the holiday? _____

2. When is it celebrated?_____

3. What is the origin (history) of the holiday? _____

   _____

   _____

4. What is the purpose of the holiday? _____

   _____

   _____

5. What do people do on the holiday? _____

_____

_____

6. Are there any special foods for the holiday? _____

_____

_____

7. Are there any special symbols or decorations for the holiday? _____

_____

_____

8. What's the best thing about this holiday? _____

_____

_____

activity three

Writing a First Draft

Use the answers to the questions in activity two to write a few paragraphs about your holiday. Use these four guidelines to help you to write. Your teacher can also help you.

1. You will probably put the information in questions 1 and 2 in the first paragraph, and the information in 3 and 4 in the second paragraph.

2. You might have one paragraph about what people do to celebrate the holiday and one about what they eat; or, that information might all be put in the same paragraph. It depends on how much you have to say.

3. A good place for the information in question 8 is in the conclusion.

4. Add the sentence with your main idea that you wrote in activity one. You will probably put this sentence at the end of your first paragraph. Your teacher can help you with this.

Giving Feedback

When you finish writing, exchange papers with another classmate. (Your teacher may ask more than one person to read your paper—and for you to read more than one paper!)

First, edit your classmate's paper. Look for and correct these things:

- Is there anything that isn't clear in the paper? Write your questions in the margin.

- Are there any mistakes in grammar or spelling? If something doesn't look right but you are not sure whether to change it, ask your teacher for help.

Writing a Second Draft

Now, return your papers. Write your final draft, using your classmate's feedback.

- Look at the grammar and spelling corrections. If you think they are right, change them; if you are not sure, ask your teacher.

- Read the questions that are written in the margin. Write some sentences that answer these questions. Add these sentences to your paper where they make sense.

A Step Beyond

Bring in items you use to celebrate the holiday that you wrote about in this chapter. These can be clothing, decorations, food, or other items. Show them to the class and explain how they are used in the celebration. If you can bring in some food that is important to your celebration, share it with the class and explain its importance.

CHAPTER eleven

Science and Technology

in this chapter

Technology is changing our lives: the way we learn, the way we communicate, even the way we have fun. In this chapter, you will talk and read about some new developments in communications technology. The video segment shows some educational multi-media products, including an encyclopedia on a CD-ROM. You will plan your own CD-ROM product, and write a letter to a multimedia company describing your product.

161

Getting Ready

activity one

Warming Up

Discuss the following questions with your class or in small groups.

1. On the whole, do you think new technology is making our lives easier or harder? Give an example.

2. Do you think that technology is bringing people together or making us have less contact with each other? Give examples.

3. Do you use technology more than your parents (or people of their generation), less, or about the same?

Asking Questions About Technology

activity two

You are going to find out which classmates have used some aspects or products of new technology. Interview your classmates using the questions here and on the next page. Ask each classmate a different question. Fill in the chart, following the example. When your teacher asks you, report on why your classmates liked or didn't like using these examples of technology.

Have you ever . . .	Name	When/How Often?	Did You Like It?	Why or Why Not?
watched a movie on a laser videodisc?	Julio	about once a week	yes	no commercials
used an Automatic Teller Machine at a bank?				
used a computer at school?				
used a computer at home or at work?				
used a cellular telephone?				

Have you ever . . .	Name	When/How Often?	Did You Like It?	Why or Why Not?
listened to music on a compact disc (CD) player?				
sent e-mail?				
sent or received a fax?				
used a word processor to write a paper for school?				

Reading About CD-ROMs

Exploring Words

CD stands for compact disc. You have probably seen music CDs—small shiny disks that play in special machines and produce very good sound quality. CD-ROMs for computers look just like music CDs, but they store pictures and words as well as sounds. ROM stands for Read Only Memory. That means that, just like music CDs, you can't record anything new on them; you can only watch and listen to what is already recorded. Computers with CD-ROM drives are becoming popular because CDs can store much more information than smaller 3-$\frac{1}{2}$" floppy disks.

Discuss the following words with your teacher or look them up in your dictionary before you read the passage.

debacle	images
unfortunately	plug in
illustrated	undoubtedly
encyclopedia	suspicious

Reading

Read the following article. Some of the words in the article have numbers below them. You will study these words after the reading.

The Great Multimedia Debacle

A   Christmas 1994 has been called the "great multimedia debacle." It was supposed to be the year that families in the United States would finally see how computer technology could provide entertainment and education for everyone through the use of multimedia.

B   "Multimedia" describes an information technology that uses text, pictures, and sound together. Usually this technology is interactive¹—the person(s) using the equipment can input information. Computer games in video arcades are probably the best known form of multimedia, but they usually use cartoon-like² pictures instead of real video and photographic images³. Before the early 1990s, most computers didn't have the storage space for video and sound, or the ability to show high quality pictures. But in 1994, several computer companies offered multimedia "packages"—computers with CD-ROM drives, television-quality screens, and speakers for sound—for under $2,000. Also, a wide range of good CD-ROM entertainment and educational programs became available, including games, encyclopedias, and interactive novels where the computer user can make choices that change the story.

C   Unfortunately, none of it worked quite as well as it looked in the TV commercials.[4] People bought the multimedia equipment thinking that they could just plug it in and go. Instead, they often needed to add extra equipment and software to their computers to make the CDs work. Many of the CDs, manufactured by different companies than the computers, had mistakes that made them stop in the middle or give strange error messages. And many of the CDs were just stories with some pictures added—not much different from illustrated books.

D   Thousands of people who bought multimedia systems for their children for Christmas took them back to the store in January. They complained the computers were too hard to use or didn't do what they expected.

E   Undoubtedly, the hardware and software companies are improving[5] their products. After all, the first home computers in the early 1980s only had two kilobytes of memory while today's computers often[6] have over 4,000 times that amount. The question is: Does the average consumer believe the companies when they say that they've solved the problems of 1994? Or will consumers remain suspicious of multimedia for some time to come?

Understanding the Reading

Discussing the Reading

activity one

In groups or with the class, discuss the following questions about the reading.

1. Why do you think people were interested in the multimedia computers?

2. What went wrong with the multimedia computers and the CDs?

3. Have you ever bought something and found that it wasn't what you expected?

Exploring Words

Use the vocabulary words from page 164 to fill in the blanks in the following sentences.

1. The computer companies were _____ happy when so many people bought multimedia packages before Christmas.

2. _____, many of those people returned the computers, so the companies ended up losing money.

3. You have to make sure you know where to _____ the CD-ROM drive on the back of the computer or it won't work.

4. Most children's books are _____ while books for adults are often just text.

5. The _____ stored on CD-ROMs can be photographs, drawings, or moving pictures.

6. If you want to read about the history of computers, you'll have to look in an _____, not a dictionary.

7. Some people are _____ of the claims that computer software can be educational.

8. Another _____ like the Christmas of 1994, and some computer companies may go out of business.

Using Adverbs

> Adverbs can modify verbs, adjectives, or entire sentences. For example, in the sentence "Barbara drove quickly down the street," the word *quickly* tells how she drove. But in the sentence "Luckily, there was little traffic, so she arrived on time," the word *luckily* applies to the whole sentence.

The following adverbs are numbered in the story. Find each one and decide whether it modifies a single word or the whole sentence. Write the word or sentence on the lines.

Adverb	Word or Sentence Modified
1. usually	_____
2. probably	_____
3. usually	_____
4. unfortunately	_____
5. undoubtedly	_____
6. only	_____

Writing About New Technology

activity four

One of the most important effects of new technology is how it allows people all over the world to share information quickly and easily. As a class or in small groups, make a list of new inventions or developments in communications technology. Discuss how each of them allows people to share information quickly and easily.

What invention or development in modern technology has had the greatest effect on your life? Write a short essay that describes the technology and how it has affected you. What has the technology allowed you to do? Why is this important? How might your life be different without this technology?

Watching a Video "CD-ROMs"

Preparing to Watch

You are going to watch a video that shows some educational multimedia, including an encyclopedia on CD-ROM. The story is from 1992. Remember that technology changes quickly, so some of the multimedia products shown in the story are already old-fashioned.

activity one

Discuss the following questions in small groups.

1. Would you rather learn something new by reading about it or watching a TV show about it?

2. Do you learn new words in English better by reading them or by hearing someone say them?

3. Do you prefer to write letters to people or to talk to them on the telephone?

Why do you think people have different answers to questions 1 to 3?

activity two

Exploring Words

Before viewing the video, discuss the terms below with your teacher and the class. As you watch, notice how these words and phrases are used.
encyclopedia

the blink of an eye   impressive
the MTV generation   skyrocket
fascinating

First Viewing: Listening for General Information

activity three

As you watch the video, think about the answers to the following questions:

1. How useful do you think CD-ROMs are for learning?

2. How is an encyclopedia on CD-ROM different from a printed encyclopedia?

3. What are the different CD-ROMs shown in the video? Briefly describe each one.

4. In what ways do the CDs shown in the video look "old-fashioned?"

5. Tell your teacher any unfamiliar words you remember hearing on the video. She or he can write them on the board. When you watch the second time, check to see if you hear the same words again.

Second Viewing: Listening for Specific Information

activity four

Listen for the nine words and phrases on the next page. Some are idioms, while others are *jargon*—special words used by people who work with computers. Try to guess what each one means from the way it is used in the video. Match each word or phrase with the appropriate definition on the right. Write the letters of the definitions on the lines.

Word or Phrase	Definition
1. _____ industry standard	a. number of people who have a CD-ROM player
2. _____ jazz up the computer	b. ability for the user to make choices
3. _____ the hottest thing	c. amazing, surprising things
4. _____ in the blink of an eye	d. people who have grown up watching music videos
5. _____ install base	e. pretending to be something else
6. _____ in the guise of	f. the newest, most exciting thing
7. _____ interactivity	g. very quickly
8. _____ gee whiz stuff	h. add interesting, exciting elements
9. _____ the MTV generation	i. most commonly used

Now, which three words/phrases do you think are jargon—words specific to the computer industry?

1. _____

2. _____

3. _____

Third Viewing: Listening for Numerical Information

activity five

Watch the video again. Listen for the following information and write the numbers in the spaces.

1. A CD-ROM stores _____ times as much information as a standard computer disk.

2. A CD-ROM can hold _____ pages of information.

3. The Compton's Encyclopedia on CD-ROM has _____ articles and _____ photographs.

4. The print version of the encyclopedia comes in _____ volumes.

5. The install base of CD-ROM players in 1992 was about _____. It was expected to _____ by 1993 and to be _____ by 1995.

Designing a Multimedia CD-ROM

Planning a Project

activity one

What would you put on a CD if you could make your own? Follow these instructions to plan a multimedia application.

1. Work in pairs or groups of three.

2. First, decide what kind of CD you are going to plan: educational, entertainment, business, or some other type. You might design a CD-ROM for learning English, for playing a game, for learning how to do a particular job, or on any other topic that interests you.

3. Now, decide what information you would use. You don't need to know the exact information, just describe what you want your CD to do.

4. How would your CD-ROM work? Use the questions below to describe how it would work.
   a. Would you present the information in written word, spoken word, or both?
   b. What pictures, drawings, moving pictures, or other images would you use?
   c. What music or other sound would you use?
   d. How would the user interact with the video?

Selling Your Product

activity two

Each group will make a poster to sell their CD-ROMs to the other students. Use the information that you generated in activity one to prepare a poster about your multimedia CD. Follow the instructions for preparing and presenting a poster from Chapter Ten, but remember that the purpose of the poster is to sell your CD. Set a price, and see how many students agree to "buy" your CD-ROM.

Writing a Proposal Letter

activity three

Suppose you want to have a multimedia company produce and sell your multimedia application. You would start by writing a proposal letter to the company, describing your CD. Write a letter to the company below, asking them to produce your CD. Use the example of a business letter in Chapter

Four to help you format your letter correctly. The content should contain the following things:

1. Introduce yourself.

2. Describe your CD: Explain what the purpose of the CD is, what sounds and pictures it would have, how the user would interact with the CD.

3. Tell who you think would buy your CD.

4. Ask the company to get in touch with you if they are interested. Give your phone number and return address so they can respond.

Write to: Bill Appleton
President
Cyberflix, Inc.
Knoxville, Tennessee 12345

A Step Beyond

Visit a store that sells computer software. Look at the CD-ROMS. Then, write a short report about what you learned, using the answers to the questions below.

1. About how many educational CD-ROMs did you see in the store? How many did you see for entertainment purposes (games, etc.)? How many for businesses? Other?

2. What kinds of educational CDs did you see?

3. How many CD-ROMs did you see for young children? How many for high school students? University students? Adults?

4. If you saw a CD demonstrated, what did you like about it? What didn't you like?

CHAPTER twelve

You, the Consumer

Some people only shop when they need something specific. Others shop as a form of recreation. When and why do you shop? You are going to read about spenders and savers in the United States. You will do an activity to see the difference between a necessity and a luxury, and interview people about their shopping habits. The video segment is about one of the biggest shopping days of the year in the United States—the day after Thanksgiving. Finally, you'll compare information on some cars and write a recommendation about which car to buy.

Getting Ready

Warming Up

 Discuss the following questions with your class or in small groups.

1. Have you been to shopping centers or malls where many different stores, restaurants, and (sometimes) movie theaters are under the same roof, as in the picture above? Where?

2. Do people often use credit cards to buy clothing in your native culture? Do they use them in restaurants? To pay for car repairs? To buy plane tickets?

3. Teenagers in North America spend a lot of time in big shopping centers. They meet friends in malls, eat there, go to the movies, and just "hang out." In countries or cities that don't have big shopping malls, where do teenagers meet and socialize?

4. If you have been to a shopping center in North America, did you notice anything that was unfamiliar to you? What things are similar to the shopping centers in your native country? What things are different?

Reading About Consumers

Reading

Read the following piece about spenders and savers. As you read, think about these questions:

1. Is it always bad to spend money? Is it always good to save money?

2. What happens to the money that people save in banks?

3. What should people think about when deciding whether to spend or save money?

Spender or Saver?

A   Is it better for people to spend their money or save it? That's not an easy question to answer. In the United States, one sign of a good economy is when consumers spend a lot of money and buy expensive items such as televisions, video cameras, computers, jewelry, and other luxury items. Experts talk about "consumer confidence." This means that when people feel good about their jobs and are able to pay their bills, they buy more things. That means that factories have to produce more, so they hire more employees. These employees then earn money that they can use to buy things. And so it continues, with more spending resulting in more jobs.

B However, it is also good for the economy when people save money. Money saved in banks is loaned to other people to start new businesses or improve businesses. This way, more people have jobs. Sometimes the money is loaned to people to buy houses. This gives jobs to the workers who design and build homes. If banks don't have any money to lend, the economy can't grow and some people will be out of work. Then they can't even buy necessities such as food and clothing.

C When people spend too much money and save too little, it can be bad for their own financial security and for their country's economy. So as a consumer, you have to make a serious decision: How much money should you spend and how much should you save? It's an important decision for your future and for the future of your country.

Understanding the Reading

Exploring Words

R W
activity one

Read the definitions below. In each paragraph, find a word (or words) that matches the definition. Write the word(s) on the line after each paragraph letter.

Definitions	Paragraph	
1. belief that the economy will be good in the future	A	_____
2. something you don't really need	A	_____
3. things you must have to live	B	_____
4. being certain of having enough money in the future	C	_____

Necessity vs. Luxury

Obviously, people have to spend money on those things they need to live, especially food, clothing, and a place to live. If they want to save money, they usually do it by buying fewer luxuries. But one person's necessities may be another person's luxuries.

activity two

Answer the following questions on your own. Then form small groups and compare your answers. If you have different answers, discuss why they are different.

1. What do you think is the difference between a necessity and a luxury?

_____

_____

_____

2. Rank the 16 items below. Put 1 by the item that is most important to you: a real necessity. Put 16 by the item that is least important to you: a real luxury. Rank all the other items between 1 and 16.

_____ a television

_____ a radio

_____ a microwave oven

_____ a car

_____ a bicycle

_____ a VCR

_____ a computer

_____ a washing machine

_____ a clothes dryer

_____ a telephone

_____ a dishwasher

_____ a wristwatch

_____ air conditioner

_____ central heat

_____ a college education for each child in your family

_____ a separate bedroom for each child in your family

activity three

Saving Money

Suppose you had $100 a month to put in a savings account. Name three things you think are worth saving for. How long would it take you to save enough money to buy your three things?

Write down the information. Then discuss it with your classmates.

Watching a Video "Shopping"

Preparing to Watch

activity one

Before you watch the video, answer these questions with your class or in small groups.

1. These signs may sometimes appear in store windows. What do they mean? At what time(s) of the year might you see them?

2. In the United States, one of biggest shopping days of the year is the day after Thanksgiving (the third Thursday in November). Why do you think this is? Would you like to shop on this day?

First Viewing: Listening for General Information

activity two

The video is about shopping on the day after Thanksgiving. The camera will focus on five different speakers (*Speakers A-E*). As you watch, think about who they are and how they feel. Then answer the following questions. Circle the best answer.

1. Where do you think the speakers are?

   a. at a large shopping mall

   b. downtown

   c. at a discount store

2. Four of the speakers are shoppers. Which speaker is a salesperson? How do you know?

   A   B   C   D   E

3. Four of the speakers seem happy. Which one is not?

   A   B   C   D   E

4. Which speaker likes the Christmas music?

   A   B   C   D   E

5. Which speaker plans to spend all day shopping?

   A   B   C   D   E

6. Which speaker is looking for a pair of earrings?

   A   B   C   D   E

Second Viewing: Listening for Specific Information

activity three

This time, listen more carefully to what the five speakers say. Try to fill in the missing words below.

Speaker A:

"Everything's on _____ and it kinda makes you feel good. Everything's Christmassy. You know, you hear the Christmas music every-where and everything. It's just a really _____ day to shop."

Speaker B:

"We're out here for the sales, the specials, and the _____,

and, uh, all day _____."

Speaker C:

"We've got great merchandise in the _____ right

now. We've got _____ sales associates to help out any-

body that needs help."

Speaker D:

"So far she says the shopping's been pretty good, in fact. 25% off.

_____% off. Good _____."

Speaker E:

"No, I'm not having _____. I'm spending

_____. That's—that's not my idea of

_____."

Writing About Shopping

activity four

What's your favorite time or place to go shopping? Do you think shopping
is a pleasant recreational activity or do you only shop when you really need
something? Write and explain your answers in a paragraph. Then, read your
answers to the class. How many people enjoy shopping?

Interviewing and Taking a Poll

activity one

Interviewing

You're going to interview three people who live in your area to find out how they feel about shopping. Ask the questions in the chart and fill in the answers.

Shopping Mall Poll	1	2	3
1. How often do you go shopping?			
2. Do you shop for fun or only when you need to?			
3. Do you look for sales when you shop?			
4. Do you look at ads in the newspaper to find sales?			
5. Do you watch TV ads (commercials) to find sales?			
6. Do you prefer big department stores or small specialty shops?			
7. Do you like to shop in a mall?			
8. What else do you do in a mall besides shop?			
9. Do you usually pay cash for things or do you use a credit card?			
10. What is your favorite kind of store?			

Analyzing Data

Discuss the results of the poll in your class. Add up the answers to each question. Make sentences using percentages. For example, you have 20 students in your class, and 15 people answered "yes" to question 3. You can write: *Seventy-five percent of the people said that they look for sales.*

Write more sentences with percentages below

_____

_____

_____

_____

_____

_____

_____

_____

_____

Role Play

Role play some shopping situations. Follow these instructions:

1. Work in pairs.

2. Choose one of the three situations.

3. Create a conversation with your partner. You can either write it or improvise—make it up as you go.

4. Tape your conversation or perform it for the class.

5. Here are some expressions you might want to use in your conversations.

"Would you show me . . .?"

"May I see . . . ?"

"I need a bigger one (smaller one, longer one, shorter one, cheaper one, etc.)."

"Do you have anything less expensive (more attractive, easier to carry, with better sound, etc.)?"

"I wasn't planning to spend that much."

"That wasn't exactly what I had in mind.

Situation 1

Student A, customer: You are looking for a computer. You have $1500 to spend. You would like a computer with a CD-ROM drive so you can use multimedia applications.

Student B, clerk: You sell computers in a store. You have three different computers to sell.

a. A Dac-tel with a CD-ROM drive and a color monitor: $2,300.

b. An Orange Produca with a CD-ROM drive and a color monitor: $1,300.

c. An Apex with a color monitor, $1,300/Separate CD-ROM drive: $250.

Situation 2

Student A, customer: You want to buy a small stereo to play your cassettes and CDs. You have $200 to spend.

Student B, clerk: You sell television and stereos. You have three different stereos to sell. You make more money if you sell the expensive stereos.

a. CD and cassette player: $400. Very good sound quality.

b. CD and cassette player: $195. Mediocre sound quality.

c. Cassette player only $150. Excellent sound quality. CD player that can be added: $100.

Situation 3

Student A, customer: You want to buy a souvenir to send to your mother or a friend. You have no idea what to buy. You want to spend between $30 and $50.

Student B, clerk: You have some nice souvenirs to sell. You make more money if you sell the expensive ones.

a. A beautiful bowl, handmade by local artists: $60.

b. A silver ring with a stone that came from the local area: $40.

c. A framed picture of a local attraction: $30.

d. A coffee cup with the name of the city on the side: $5.

Using a Consumer Guide

Reading

activity one

Imagine that you were asked to recommend a car for a family to buy. Read the information below about the Ramírez family.

A   Olga and Carlos Ramírez are in their early 30s. They have two children, ages 5 and 2. At least twice a year, they take the children to see their grandparents, a trip of 600 miles each way. Otherwise, Carlos drives five miles to work each day. They use the car on weekends to go shopping, visit friends, and go to recreation areas just outside the city.

B   Olga and Carlos need a car that will be powerful enough to drive on the highways for their long trips. It must be economical to drive around the city and big enough for their family as the children get older. They need a car with four doors to make it easy to put the two-year-old in her carseat, and they prefer a car with large trunk space. They also want an AM/FM radio, cassette player, and air conditioning. They have decided that they can afford to spend between $13,000 and $15,000, but would prefer to spend as little as possible.

184   INTERACTIONS ONE: A Multi-Skills Activity Book

Reading a Chart

Look at the information in the chart below. Then answer the questions that follow with a partner. When you finish, compare answers with other classmates.

1. Which car gets the best gas mileage? (Good gas mileage means they will spend less money on gasoline.)

2. Which car has the best warranty?

3. Which car has the most room for luggage?

4. Which car has the most powerful engine for long-distance driving?

5. Which car is most expensive? Least expensive?

	Mazda 626	Ford Escort	Toyota Corolla	Chevrolet Corsica	Nissan Sentra
A/C	yes	yes	yes	yes	yes
AM/FM Radio-Cassette	yes	yes	yes	yes	yes
Four-door model	yes	yes	yes	yes	yes
Hatchback	no	yes	no	yes	no
Gas Mileage	24 city 31 highway	26 city 34 highway	30 city 35 highway	25 city 35 highway	27 city 35 highway
Engine Size	2.2 liters	1.9 liters	1.6 liters	2.0 liters	1.6 liters
Trunk Space	15 cubic feet	17.7 cubic feet	26.1 cubic feet	13.5 cubic feet	24 cubic feet
Warranty, in years	3 years, 50,000 miles	6 years, 60,000 miles	3 years, 36,000 miles	3 years, 50,000 miles	3 years, 36,000 miles
Price	$15,000– $16,000	$12,000– $13,500	$13,000– $14,000	$12,500– $13,500	$11,000– $12,000

Notes: *A/C* means air conditioning.

A *hatchback* is a type of car with a door that opens up in the back of the car.

Gas mileage is the number of miles the car will go on one gallon of gas.

The engine size is a measure of how powerful the car is; the larger the engine size, the more powerful the engine.

The warranty tells the period of time or number of miles that the company will pay for certain types of repairs to the engine or body of the car.

The price varies, depending on extras and how well the buyer deals with the salesperson.

Writing a Recommendation

Write a recommendation, telling the Ramírez family which car you think they should buy. First, complete the following sentence. Do *not* use any numbers in the first sentence.

I recommend that you buy a _____

because_____

_____

Now add information about all the features of the car that you are recommending and explain how that feature will help the Ramírez family. For example,

Feature

The Escort has a hatchback.

Benefit

This will make it easy to load the groceries and luggage.

Add a concluding sentence that summarizes the information about the car. Now, write your complete recommendation. Use the sentences your wrote above. Add anything you need to connect the sentences into paragraphs.

Comparing Recommendations

Form groups of three or four. Compare your recommendations. Did you all recommend the same car? If not, why did you recommend different cars?

If you chose different cars, think of some questions you could ask Olga and Carlos Ramírez to find out which car would be best for them. Write your questions below:

_____

_____

_____

_____

A Step Beyond

activity one

Work with a partner. Ask your partner some questions to find something that your partner would like to have: a car, a stereo, a camera, a computer, or something else. Find out what features your partner wants this item to have. Then, do some research. Visit some stores or go to the library for some consumer information. Write a recommendation: Tell your partner which one to buy.

activity two

Look at some ads in a newspaper for computers, cars, or stereo equipment. Compare the ads. What facts do the ads give you about the items? What do the ads do to *persuade* you to buy the items? Can newspaper ads help you to be a smart consumer? Discuss the answers to these questions with your partner.

Answer Key

CHAPTER one

Working with Third Person Singular,
Activity Two, p. 4
1. doesn't have
2. works
3. helps
4. wants
5. doesn't want

WATCHING A VIDEO:

First Viewing, Activity Two, p. 7
1. Brooklyn
2. English as a Second Language
3. pharmacy studies
4. getting larger

Second Viewing, Activity Four, p. 8
1. 700
2. 16
3. 1-3

Third Viewing, Activity Five, p. 8
1. c.
2. a.
3. e.
4. b.
5. d.

CHAPTER **two**

Reading, Activity Two, p. 13
1. B
2. D
3. A
4. C

Understanding the Reading, Activity One, p. 14
1. produce
2. wind

3. survive
4. oxygen
5. tornado
6. melt

Understanding Reference, Activity Two, p. 14
1. some parts of the world
2. plants and animals
3. tornado
4. tornadoes
5. on the road
6. windmills like this one
7. many different kinds of plants
8. funnel-shaped cloud
9. snow along this mountain road

WATCHING A VIDEO:

First Viewing, Activity Three, p. 19
1. A
2. B
3. C
4. B, C

Second Viewing, Activity Four, p. 20
1. age: 9 years
   weight: 400 pounds
   kind of bear: Black Bear
2. b.
3. a. Sunday
   b. morning
   c. 5:00
4. a.
5. b.

Working with Grammar, Activity One, pp. 25–26
1. There is a problem in Southville.
2. There are not enough runways at the airport.
3. There are wetlands west of the airport.
4. It is important to build a new runway.
5. It is necessary to save the wetlands.
6. Is it possible for both sides to agree?
7. The planes can't take off or land on time.
8. Southville may lose new businesses.

9. Many plants and animals will die without the wetlands.
10. The government is trying to save the wetlands.
11. The people of Southville are discussing a solution.

CHAPTER three

WATCHING A VIDEO:

First Viewing, Activity Three, p. 37
1. Healthy Dining in San Diego
2. A news reporter
   An employee of El Pollo Loco
   A customer at El Pollo Loco
   The regional manager of Jack-in-the-Box
   A customer at Jack-in-the-Box
3. El Pollo Loco
   Wendy's
   Taco Bell
   La Salsa
   Jack-in-the-Box

Second Viewing, Activity Four, p. 38
1. 2,000
2. 66
3. 88
4. fried, buttery, creamy, sauces, cheeses

Applying Your Knowledge, Activity Five, p. 38
Low Fat: beans, flame-broiled chicken, rice, chicken teriyaki bowl
High Fat: taco, french fries, colossus burger, milkshakes

Skimming for Main Ideas, Activity Two, p. 39
1. C
2. D
3. A
4. E
5. B

Exploring Words, Activity One, p. 41
1. came out with
2. switched
3. by the score
4. labeled
5. lean
6. gorgeous
7. latest
8. forever

Understanding Reference, Activity Two, pp. 41–42
1. scientists
2. people in the United States

3. bran muffins (two times)
4. food items
5. cholesterol
6. food products
7. pasta and potatoes
8. become lean and gorgeous

CHAPTER four

Reading, Activity Three, pp. 47-49
1. D
2. A
3. C
4. B

Exploring Words, Activity Two, p. 50
1. muggy
2. high-rise
3. hike
4. advantages
5. dawn
6. check on
7. crowds
8. close by

WATCHING A VIDEO:

First Viewing, Activity Two, p. 52
1. No
2. Interview people at the Festival
3. *Answers will vary; some possible answers:*
   Eating, selling things, drinking, walking around, playing games of chance, having a good time

Second Viewing, Activity Three, p. 52
1. d.
2. c.
3. a.
4. b.

Third Viewing, Activity Four, p. 52
1. games of chance
2. baseball toss
3. forty-fourth
4. Canal to Grant
5. She's a shy one.

CHAPTER five

Matching, Activity One, p. 64
1. c.

2. b.
3. e
4. d
5. a.

Working with Verbs and Transition Words,
Activity Four, p. 66

Paragraph A: but: contrasting; also: additional; then: time
Paragraph B: first: time; or: choice; next: time; then: time
Paragraph C: but: contrasting; then: time
Paragraph D: finally: time; now: time

WATCHING A VIDEO:

First Viewing, Activity Three, p. 68
1. a news reporter; a mortgage company employee
2. Generation Link
3. California

Second Viewing, Activity Four, p. 68
1. a relative
2. 0%
3. home equity
4. $20,000 to $203,000
5. the buyer
6. six

CHAPTER six

Talking About Emergencies, Activity One, p. 82
1. b, e, g
2. d, h, n
3. a, f, i
4. c, j, l
5. k, m, o

Using Transition Words, Activity Two, p. 83
1. *so:* Often the wind blows the snow around so that it is impossible to see.
2. *also:* They also occur in the Pacific, where they are called typhoons.
3. *then:* Then, water overflows the banks of the river.
4. *for example:* For example, in the northeastern part of the United States there are few strong earthquakes.

WATCHING A VIDEO:

First Viewing, Activity Three, p. 85
1. New York's JFK airport
2. Kobe, Japan
3. Two
4. The young man

Second Viewing, Activity Four, p. 85
1. 280
2. 1.4
3. 15,000.
4. 10:35 A.M.
5. a. Japanese Consulate: 212 371-8222
     b. U.S. Department of Defense: 703 057-5737
6. a. Japanese Consulate
     b. U.S. State Department
     c. U.S. Department of Defense

CHAPTER seven

All questions in this chapter are open-ended; accordingly, answers will vary.

CHAPTER eight

Warming Up, Activity, p. 116
Television: anchors, reporters, commercials, cable channel, sitcom (perhaps editorials)
Movies/Films: theater, flick
Newspapers: columnists, reporters, editorials, advertisements
Radio: DJs, reporters, commercials (perhaps editorials)
On-line computer service: interactive, bulletin boards, e-mail

Thinking About the Reading, Activity One,
pp. 118-119
1. pay-per-preview movies; computer or video games; "video mall" shopping
2. You have to phone the company when you want to pause a movie, then punch in a code and wait up to a minute for the movie to pause.

Using a Prefix to Make Opposites, Activity Four,
p. 119
1. unimportant
2. unhappy
3. undependable
4. unbelievable
5. unconscious,
6. unafraid
7. unfortunate

WATCHING A VIDEO:

Preparing to Watch, Activity One, p. 120
black and white picture, rooftop antenna, small screen, snowy picture

Listening for General Information, Activity Four, p. 121

1. b.
2. a.
3. c.

CHAPTER **nine**

Thinking About the Reading, Activity One, p. 133

1. b
2. c
3. d
4. a

Matching, Activity Two, p. 134

1. Gabe Essic
2. Gabe Essic
3. Jill Hammond
4. Gabe Essic
5. Darrin Wells

WATCHING A VIDEO:

Second Viewing, Activity Three, p. 136

Jim Sulas:

"Looking confident is important."

"Men should dress well to attract well-dressed women."

Victoria Parker:

"Think positive thoughts, not negative ones."

"Do things you enjoy and you'll attract people."

"Women sometimes expect too much from their dates."

Judy Knowle:

"Creative ads work best."

"If you write negative things, you'll attract negative people."

Third Viewing, Activity Four, p. 137

Possible answers:

Like: aura of confidence, positive thinking, men being well-dressed

Don't Like: negative thinking, someone trying to impress you, men complimenting women's body parts, using the same lines, saying the same things, women who become "clingers," women who expect too much, questions like: "What kind of car do you drive? How much money do you have?"

CHAPTER **ten**

Exploring Words, Activity One, p. 150

1. understand
2. connect
3. protect
4. tragedy
5. defend
6. values

Finding the Main Ideas, Activity Three, p. 151

1. D
2. C
3. B
4. E
5. A

WATCHING A VIDEO:

First Viewing, Activity Three, p. 152

Questions are open-ended. Answers will vary.

Second Viewing, Activity Four, pp. 152–153

1. The woman in the curlers: "What I like about the parade, it's part of our culture. It teaches the young children our culture."
2. The man with the cap: What I like and enjoy most is seeing the kids participating and dancing and a variety of our African-American brothers and sisters coming down and showing what our community is made of—positive stuff.
3. Narrator: Marchers relax from all that walking by shopping at a vendors' market set up especially for this day filled with African goods.

Matching, Activity One, pp. 153–155

1. Independence Day
2. Halloween
3. Thanksgiving
4. Presidents' Day
5. Memorial Day
6. New Year's Day

CHAPTER eleven

Exploring Words, Activity Two, p. 166
1. undoubtedly
2. Unfortunately
3. plug in
4. illustrated
5. images
6. encyclopedia
7. suspicious
8. debacle

Using Adverbs, Activity Three, p. 166
1. Usually this technology is interactive—the person(s) using the equipment can input information.
2. are
3. use
4. Unfortunately, none of it worked quite as well as it looked in the TV commercials.
5. Undoubtedly, the hardware and software companies are improving their products.
6. have

WATCHING A VIDEO:

First Viewing, Activity Three, p. 168
Discussion questions. Accept all answers.

Second Viewing, Activity Four, p. 169

1. industry standard   i. most commonly used (jargon)
2. jazz up the   h. add interesting, exciting
   computer   elements
3. the hottest thing   f. the newest, most exciting thing
4. in the blink of an   g. very quickly
   eye
5. install base   a. number of people who have a
                           CD ROM player (jargon)
6. in the guise of   e. pretending to be something else
7. interactivity   b. ability for the user to make
                           choices (jargon)
8. gee whiz stuff   c. amazing, surprising things
9. the MTV   d. people who have grown up
   generation   watching music videos

The three jargon words/phrases:
1. industry standard
2. install base
3. interactivity

Third Viewing, Activity Five, p. 169
1. 500
2. 200,000
3. 33,000 articles and 13,000 photographs
4. 26 volumes
5. 2 million in 1992, double by 1993, 8 million by 1995

CHAPTER twelve

Exploring Words, Activity One, p. 176
1. consumer confidence
2. luxury
3. necessities
4. financial security

WATCHING A VIDEO:

First Viewing, Activity Two, p. 179
1. a.
2. C (refers to store as "we," talks about what store can offer shoppers)
3. E
4. A
5. B
6. D

Second Viewing, Activity Three, pp. 179–180
Speaker A: sale, good
Speaker B: bargains, shopping
Speaker C: store, lots of
Speaker D: 10%, sales
Speaker E: fun, money, fun

Grateful acknowledgment is made for the use of the following:

Photographs: *Page 1* © Sally Gati; *3* © K. Preuss/The Image Works; *11* © Sally Gati; *13 (top three)* © Sally Gati; *13 (bottom)* © Dewey Bergquist/Monkmeyer; *15 (all)* © Sally Gati; *23 (left)* © Michael Hubrich/Photo Researchers; *23 (right)* © Jeff Albertson/Stock Boston; *29* © Sally Gati; *36 (left)* © Sally Gati; *36 (right)* © Eunice Harris/Photo Researchers; *45* © Mike Kagan/Monkmeyer; *48 (top)* © N. R. Rowan/Stock Boston; *48 (middle)* © Bohdan Hrynewych/Stock Boston; *48 (bottom)* © Sally Gati; *49* © James Blank/Stock Boston; *53 (dentist)* Joel Gordon; *53 (all but dentist)* © Sally Gati; *61* © Walter Gilardetti; *77* © Spencer Grant/Photo Researchers; *79 (top)* © Timothy Marshall/Liaison International; *79 (bottom)* © Barbara Alper/Stock Boston; *80 (top)* © Nita Winter/Image Works; *80 (bottom)* © AP Photo/Wilmington Star-News, Tyler Hicks; *81* © Adam Jones/Photo Researchers; *97* © Spencer Grant/Picture Cube; *103* © Toni Michaels/Image Works; *106* © Sally Gati; *115* © W. Hill, Jr./Image Works; *117* © Randy Taylor/Sygma; *129* © Andy Levin/Photo Researchers; *130* © Sally Gati; *147* © Salli Gati; *149 (left)* © David Austin/Stock Boston; *149 (right)* © Gary A. Conner/PhotoEdit; *161* © Diane Renda; *162* © Walter Gilardetti; *163 (left)* © Stanley Rowin/Picture Cube; *163 (right)* © Carolyn A. McKeone/Photo Researchers; *167* © Joel Gordon; *171* © Joel Gordon; *173* © Sally Gati; *174* © Walter Gilardetti; *175* © Mark Richards/PhotoEdit; *180* © Walter Gilardetti.

Text Credits: *Pages 71–72* Based on *Greater San Diego Apartment Guide,* April, 1994. Hass Publishing Company; *99* (Topic One: Second-hand Smoke) Based on *Mayo Clinic Family Health Book.* William Morrow & Co. New York, p. 412 and *Natural Health Guide to Atlanta,* Martha Ann Heller, August–September, 1980, pp. 12–13; *100* (Topic Two: The Deadliest Skin Cancer) Based on *Why You Should Know About Melanoma,* American Cancer Society, 1985 and *Newsweek* (Matt Clark with Deborah Witherspoon), June 14, 1982, p. 84; *102* (Topic Three: How to Get a Good Night's Sleep) Adapted from *American Medical Association Family Medical Guide.* 1982. Random House. New York. Pp. 20–21; *103* (Topic Four: Sexually Transmitted Diseases) Based on *Mayo Clinic Family Health Book.* William Morrow & Co. New York, p. 412 and *American Medical Association Family Medical Guide.* 1982. Random House. New York, p. 611; *110–111* From "How Vulnerable Are You to Stress," *Time* Magazine, June 6, 1983. © 1983 Time, Inc. Reprinted by permission; *123* From the Monday, August 5, 1996 *TV Guide.* Reprinted by permission of TV Guide. Copyright © 1996 News America Publications, Inc.; *132* Adapted from *The Atlanta Journal and Constitution,* Nov. 10, 1994; *143* Copyright 1994, *The Atlanta Journal and Constitution,* Taken from *The Atlanta Journal and Constitution,* Styles Section, Page 4, October 23, 1994.